The African-American Woman's Guide to
Great Sex
Happiness &
Marital Bliss

Jel D. Lewis (Jones)

Ambrosia Books
Phoenix
New York   Los Angeles

The African-American Woman's Guide to Great Sex, Happiness & Marital Bliss

by Jel D. Lewis (Jones)

Published by:
Amber Books
A Division of Amber Communication Group, Inc.
1334 East Chandler Boulevard, Suite 5-D67
Phoenix, AZ 85048
amberbk@aol.com
www.amberbooks.com

Tony Rose, Publisher/Editorial Director   Samuel P. Peabody, Associate Publisher
Yvonne Rose, Senior Editor   The Printed Page, Interior & Cover Design

The publication is designed to provide accurate and authoritative information in regard to the subject matter covered. It is sold with the understanding that the Publisher is not engaged in rendering legal, accounting or other professional services. If legal advice or other expert assistance is required, the services of a competent professional person should be sought.

AMBER BOOKS are available at special discounts for bulk purchases, sales promotions, fund raising or educational purposes.

© Copyright 2003 by Jel D. Lewis (Jones) and Amber Books
ISBN #: 0-9727519-2-0

Library of Congress Cataloging-In-Publication Data

Jones, Jel D. Lewis.
  The African-American woman's guide to great sex, happiness & marital bliss / Jel D. Lewis (Jones).
      p. cm.
  ISBN 0-9727519-2-0
1. Sex instruction for women. 2. African American women--Sexual behavior. 3. Man-woman relationships. 4. Marriage. I. Title.

HQ46 .J665 2003
306.7'089'96073—dc21

2003042665

Contents

I dedicate this book to my brother,
Willie James Jones, (deceased November, 1996) who died too young.
May this book be a remembrance to him
and all he meant to my family and I.

About the Author

Jel D. Lewis (Jones) has written and published over 100 short stories for college publications and romance magazines and nearly 200 feature articles on relationships, health, beauty, nutrition, travel and teens for leading magazines and online publications.

Currently a resident of Schaumberg, Illinois, Ms. Lewis (Jones) is a graduate of Marion College (Chicago).

Acknowledgments

I'm extremely proud of this book, but if it wasn't for the encouragement from the individuals listed on this page, it might not have been completed and published.

My most heartfelt thanks goes to Mr. Tony Rose, the CEO and publisher of Amber Books for believing in my work and this book even when I had temporarily put my own belief on the shelf.

I had looked high and low for a wonderful publisher like Amber Books and was completely excited when they accepted my manuscript.

Then, a few months after signing the book contract my life turned a depressing page. Suddenly, things took place that changed my livelihood; and suddenly, I had lost my enthusiasm to totally complete the book and do the work I needed to do.

Then one day a few months later, I decided to read my email that I had allowed to just pile up; and there I had an email from Mr. Tony Rose. He said, "Ms. Lewis (Jones) we haven't been able to reach you. We love your book and we're going ahead with it." That message was so heartwarming to me that I replied to the email and submitted my current phone and address. He called me that Sunday morning and brightened my day with the most uplifting conversation. He said to me, "We all love your work and our intentions were to go ahead with the book whether we located you or not; and hoped we could find you at some point."

I'm indebted to Sally Lee Lewis (Mom) for giving me a warm, comfortable place to live while finishing up this book and sorting out some other things in my life. And, mostly, for not letting me forget to return any phone calls from the publisher.

My most special thanks to Attorney John S. Saletta. His sincere advice gave me the encouragement that I needed to complete this book.

My deepest thanks to Mariann Grey, a co-worker who walked into my life and immediately showed me care. It was as if she wrapped a protective shield around me to protect me from any storm. If she never does another single thing for me, she has already shown me how much she cares.

My forever thanks goes to all the magazine editors who accepted my work and gave me a showcase for my writing, and who made me feel that I was writing the kind of relationship articles that people wanted to read, especially Sheila Bronner/*Upscale*, Kate Ferguson/*Today's Black Woman* and Arianne Moore/*TBW's Guide to Good Love*.

I also would like to thank all the members of my family for all their love and support of my writing.

Last, but not least, I would like to thank the man of my dreams: You know who you are!

Jel D. Lewis (Jones)

Introduction

Most of us get married for love and expect our union to last a lifetime, and we should expect that. So, it's perfect when you finally end up with that one special someone. After reading *The African-American Woman's Guide to Great Sex, Happiness and Marital Bliss*, you'll be closer to that reality.

The African-American Woman's Guide to Great Sex, Happiness & Marital Bliss is a compelling, inspiring, eye-opener. It gives you the secrets to building and maintaining a lifelong relationship by becoming the spark that ignites your mate's flame.

In simple down-to-earth terms, author Jel D. Lewis (Jones) teaches you all about true romance and open communication, and shows you how to express your love for your mate, as well as feel your mate's love in return. In this very informative and detailed marriage guide, you'll discover how to expose your inner feelings and build the foundation for a lasting relationship.

The African-American Woman's Guide to Great Sex, Happiness and Marital Bliss stresses the importance of being understood and accepted for who we are and reminds us that no matter how good our relationship is, the passion always makes it better. You'll learn how to hold onto the passion that keeps things sizzling in your love life and you'll be reminded that the backbone of a strong passionate marriage is honesty. Above all, no matter how much you love each other or want to keep your passion alive, it will never survive if you don't put forth the effort to find time for "loving." With this in mind, the author gives great relationship tips and advice in the more than thirty very informative chapters, such as: Enhance Your Sex Appeal, Communicating in Lovemaking, 13 Secrets to Sizzling Passion and 72 Ways to Love Your Lover.

According to Terrie Williams, author of *A Plentiful Harvest: Creating Balance & Harmony Through the Seven Living Virtues*, "Jel D. Lewis (Jones) gives us an easy-to-follow guideline of what we need to do truly enjoy sex, find happiness, and achieve marital bliss—all at once."

> —Yvonne Rose, author, *Is Modeling for You? The Handbook and Guide for the Aspiring Black Model*

Chapter 1

7 Ways to Love Yourself First

Are you one of those people who are quick to blame yourself for things that fall down around you? If it's broken, it must be your fault? If it's not broken, but just doesn't work, it still must be your fault? Do you take this same frame of mind into your relationships? He left so it must be your fault? If he can't love you, you must not be worth loving?

Being in a relationship that somehow goes sour sounds all too famil-iar to many of us. It's going along, but not moving along: a doomed relationship that's just stopped working all together. But to be able to keep loving yourself even when he can't, is to know you're worth loving and that just because the relationship failed doesn't mean it was your fault.

A relationship can fail or take the wrong turn for many reasons. One reason could be you're with someone who showers you with insults instead of compliments. Another reason could be you're with some-one who causes you distress instead of joy. It could be one of a hundred things. The point is your man walked out the door and whether he was the love of your life or just someone you were ready to kick to the curb, the bottom line is the bottom line—he left you.

In many situations like this, you stopped loving yourself because he stopped loving you; or maybe during the relationship he broke your spirit and you stopped loving yourself long before he even left. Don't let his leaving make you look down on yourself. Keep loving yourself; and above all, don't blame yourself for the things that were wrong with him.

Are you one of those individuals who is always trying to please your mate or other people in your life? Do you put their needs or other people's needs before your own, living for everyone but yourself? If so, according to Dr. Bryan Robinson, professor of counseling at the University of North Carolina at Charlotte, "You may have a self-esteem problem. Positive self-esteem is the cornerstone for personal happiness and healthy relationships."

If you're down because your relationship just ended, or constantly feel down on yourself regardless of the situation, here are some suggestions that may help:

Good Self-Esteem:

Good self-esteem is a state of mind. It's just like Henry Ford once said, "If you think you can or you can't, you're right." Which means your mind works sometimes according to how you program it. The starting point to achieve this effect, is to change how you think about yourself. Negative, pessimistic thinking will keep you wondering if you can, but positive thinking will tell you—you know you can. Do all you can to take yourself off of that negative road you have been traveling down. Don't allow negative thinking to undermine your self-esteem. See yourself honestly by recognizing your accomplishments along with your defeats, your strengths as well as your faults. The more you look for the positives, the better you will begin to feel about yourself.

Positive Affirmations:

Give yourself positive affirmations. Keep a notebook, scrapbook or bulletin board with the affirming letters, notes, gifts and sayings that people send you. Make a point of looking at those notes and gifts often to remind yourself of the appreciation of friends and others. Doing this will help you feel more positive about yourself. Repeating your own positive affirmations to yourself will help you feel more positive about yourself.

Stand Up for You:

Stand up to your critical inner voice. Don't allow your own self-doubt to beat you. Stand up for yourself no matter who or what is trying to put you down. Take notice of how often you put yourself down or call yourself names, then take a stand against doing that to yourself. Stand up to impossible standards and harsh judgments. Instead of attacking yourself, give yourself pep talks and learn to look at the positive side of things when the going gets rough. The bottom line is to replace that voice that you use against yourself, with one that shows you kindness and encouragement.

Befriend Yourself:

Treat yourself as your best friend. You are the best friend that you are supposed to have. You are supposed to be a rock for yourself, no matter how hard the punches. Make an all out effort to treat yourself as your very best friend, at all times, instead of looking at yourself or treating yourself like your worst enemy. Stop putting your needs last all the time, that's no way to treat a best friend. And don't make yourself a doormat for the man in your life, or others in your life. Being your best friend, means you put yourself first, taking care of your health and nutritional needs. It means you're treating yourself with respect, doing good things for yourself and surrounding yourself with people who encourage you instead of criticizing you.

Accept Limitations:

One of the hardest things for any of us to do, is learning how to accept our limitations without allowing ourselves to feel flawed or less than who we are. If you're unhappy about something you did or said, don't hold it against yourself, acknowledge that you feel bad about it and forgive yourself. Admit and accept your mistakes and forgive yourself for them. Recognize that acknowledging and accepting your vulnerabilities is a character strength, not a weakness.

Find Personal Time:

Set aside some time for yourself each day. No matter what, slice a bit of time from your busy work schedule or busy life and use it only for you. Not for your kids, not for your in-laws or your mate, just for yourself! Take these private moments to indulge yourself with some relaxing things that you enjoy, like reading, soft music, exercise or prayer. The more you give to yourself, the more deserving you feel.

Please Yourself:

Get in the habit of pleasing yourself. Pleasing others to make them happy can be an honorable thing— but not if it squeezes you out of the mix. When you trim yourself to suit everybody else, you fade yourself away until there's nothing left for you. Begin to let go of other people's opinions and form your own. Stand up for what you believe in and think is right. Don't let your spouse or anyone else take control over what you should think or believe.

Sometimes when a relationship goes sour, or when we constantly find ourselves in relationships with mates who mistreat us, we have the tendency to put up with bad treatment, thinking that maybe we deserve the treatment we are being given, because low self-esteem allows you to feel this way. There are many women who don't think that much of themselves because of bad relationships and low self-esteem. But the bottom line here is to keep loving yourself whether the person in your life loves you or not!

Chapter 2

7 Men Tell What Turns Them Off

We all know that a man can get turned on at the drop of a hat. One in a hundred things could trigger his sexual pull. Whether it's from a picture in a magazine, a heart stopping video, a certain exotic fragrance or just the way you cross your legs. But he can also get turned off just as quick. First and foremost, before any of your other traits can get an opportunity to turn him off, your looks will have to be able to turn him on! According to Dr. Joyce Brothers, author of *What Every Woman Should Know About Men*, "No matter what men say for the record, good looks are what they want most in a woman." Not that you have to look like someone off the cover of a glamorous magazine, because as we know, beauty is in the eye of the beholder. But there will have to be something about your physical appearance that catches his eye. Your figure, smooth skin, hair or your legs, just to name a few…something that he can initially see, since men are such visual people.

The average man will run from turn-offs. If there's anything about a certain woman that turns him off, he is usually nowhere around her. Because when a man gets turned off—everything shuts down. For the female who turns him off—you can get ready for his departure, he won't be hanging around too long.

Andre, 24, Gas Station Attendant

"I have had a lot of things to turn me off about former girlfriends. But what sticks out in my mind the most is the affair I had with my step-sister. My Dad remarried two years ago and the lady he married had two daughters my age. The older daughter (Tara 26) was really good-looking. She was my stepsister, but if my father could marry her mother why couldn't I marry her. We fell for each other pretty fast, I would say, and I wanted to be with her all the time. But our relation-ship didn't get off the ground too far before I started having doubts about our relationship being able to hang in there. We dated for almost a year and I ended it, because she had a thing about showing her body." He held up one finger. "No let me restate that and say, she had a thing about not showing her body. When we had sex, the lights had to be off, and she would never let me see her body with all her clothes off. The most she would take off was her underwear. Her bra always stayed on. It got to the point where I couldn't get turned on, and I knew it was not happening for us. I don't think she knew how big a turn off that was to me.

Michael, 34, Shoe Store Manager

"You probably have heard this one before, but my marriage ended because it was such a turn off to me. It got to the point that I couldn't rise to the occasion. And believe me, that's not me. Not by a long shot. I'm what you would consider a pretty passionate man, but just after one year of marriage to my ex, I got in a turned off rut and couldn't get turned back on. She was always on my back and pissed about the fact that nothing was happening in bed. Well, it wasn't my fault. I wanted to want to, but I couldn't get in the mood half the time. I knew we were headed for Splitsville. It had to do with how she trans-formed herself into some unattractive creature at night. That goop on her face and that rag she had for a nightgown. The whole time we were together, she wouldn't buy anything sexy to sleep in. She would always—without fail—come to bed dressed like my grandmother. She had nice hair down to her shoulders, but I never saw it. During the day she kept it wrapped around the top of her head in some ball and at night she slept with a hair net on. I was very much in love and the only time I would see her the way I wanted to see her with her hair down wearing a sexy see-through nightie was in my fantasies. She was a good woman, but she didn't know shit about how to keep her man happy. She turned me off so bad, until I had to leave her to keep from thinking I had a problem. You know what I mean?"

Scott, 37, School Teacher

"My biggest turn off was with Candi, who was a special woman in my life at the time. I had asked her to marry me. We were in love. I'll be honest. I fell for her eyes. She had these cat eyes; they were a cross between hazel and green. Against her dark skin, they drove me wild, along with her fine brick house body. But she had a jealousy problem that took the cake! I found out that it was really a serious problem about eight months into our relationship. She was a petite, soft-spoken female; and at first I didn't think much of it and figured I could deal with it; but that wasn't happening! Especially when I found out she was carrying a small gun in her purse at all time. I hate guns and the thought of her carrying a gun, for whatever reason, was a turn-off in itself. It was always in the back of my mind…why did she feel she needed to carry a piece? She would get upset if I glanced out the side window when a car approached with a female driver. She would get upset whenever my phone would ring. She called my job five and six times a day. She was smothering me with jealousy that gave me a permanent turn-off toward her. I ended up changing jobs and leaving town, just to get her off my ass."

Otis, 35, Convenience Store Owner

"Women who talk too much about themselves turn me off." He grinned. "But that's not what you're asking. Okay, here goes…the only woman that I can think of who really turned me off was this woman I dated for a while [three weeks] who wouldn't shave her legs or under arms. She worked the midnight shift at my store. She didn't look half bad and I knew she had a crush on me. One morning around 3:00 a.m. I purposely dropped in for something. Anyway, we locked up the store for an hour and had sex on the floor in my office. The sex with her was super, so I took her out a couple of times, but I couldn't get past all that hair on her legs and hanging from under her arms. And I didn't have the nerve to tell her that it turned me off. She doesn't know until this day why I stopped calling and taking her out. It didn't feel like my place to tell a grown woman she needs to shave."

James, 34, Landscaping
"What turned me off with a former girlfriend was something I was heavy into myself when we first met. Drinking! I used to drink pretty heavy. Debra and I met at a bar. We were both plastered the night we got together. I took her home with me and we had sex on the laundry room floor. I was still living at home at the time and didn't know company had dropped in and my mother had given them my room. To make a long story, short—we were so drunk, we didn't care where we made out. The sex was super. We started seeing each other and stayed in our relationship for a year and a half until I quit the liquid. I gave up booze because it was causing me some problems that I didn't need to deal with. I couldn't control it. After giving it up, my former girlfriend, Debra was always a turn off to me, because it got under my skin to see her like that, red eyes, sweaty face, wasted. It was so embarrassing. She would get this way in public, and on one occasion fell out of her seat at a nightclub. Once I was sober, I found that a drunk female couldn't turn me on. But seeing her like that was a reinforcement to me that I had made the right choice to give up drinking, especially since I couldn't handle it any better than she could."

Michael, 24, Mail Carrier
"What turned me off the most with a former relationship was the lie an ex-girlfriend told me. When Elaine and I started going out she told me she was 30. I knew she was older than me; but her age really didn't matter that much. What counted was that I enjoyed her company and felt comfortable and at ease with her. I thought she was pretty cool and that our relationship had possibilities. But when her daughter, who is my age, came home from college; she had to introduce me to her; but she just said, "Mike this is Peg and Peg this is Mike. In private she told me that Peg was her sister. Then a week later, when I came over looking for her, Peg answered the door and said "my mother

isn't home." That evening, Elaine came clean with me and told me that Peg was her daughter and that she was really 51. She was really sexy looking and didn't look her age at all. But after finding out, every time we had sex I kept thinking about being in bed with one of my mother's friends. That thought took away the thrill. In the beginning I was excited about dating an older woman, but after her confession, I couldn't get past dating an old woman. And when I say "old," I don't mean to offend any females out there, because being 51 definitely isn't old; but where I was standing two years ago, it seemed ancient. If she had been on the level in the beginning, maybe things would have worked out differently. So I guess it's safe to say that what really turns me off is when a woman is not truthful about her age."

Robert, 51, Engineer
"I'm divorced with two grown children, and I'm over 50 but none of my friends think I look my age; and maybe that's because I'm very much into health and fitness. And, because I'm so into health and fitness, the woman I spend any quality time with will have to be into it also. And that was the biggest turn-off I had about a former girlfriend. We met over the radio and she mentioned that she was full-figured. But what she failed to say was that she was fat. We met for coffee, and after I got over the shock of how heavy she was, I noticed I was enjoying myself; plus while sitting at the table, I couldn't see all of her, just her good-looking face and nice hair. And, after having such a nice time with her and enjoying that good night kiss, which lasted for a good fifteen minutes on her front steps, we starting seeing each other. It lasted for over four months." He paused and looked away for a second. "That was one of my miscalculations, I must say. But, I guess, in the back of my mind, I was telling myself, this woman could be a fox if she was not so damn fat. My goal was to talk her into losing about 50 pounds, because I knew deep down I wouldn't be able to keep seeing her otherwise. And she said she wanted to trim down and take care of herself, but I never did see a glimpse of her wanting to lose weight, other than talk, talk, and talk about it. Whenever we ate out, she would always eat like a pig!" He

shook his head. "Sorry, if I sound harsh, but I believe in working for what you have. I didn't break up with her because of her weight; I broke up with her because she didn't seem to care about doing anything about her weight. If she had tried wholeheartedly to diet and was unsuccessful, I would have stayed with her! All I needed to know was that she was someone who at least cared enough about herself to try."

Chapter 3

Lose Yourself in Romantic Times

Lose yourself in romantic times and allow your relationship to blossom. Even if you're not a true romantic at heart, you can still live and think as a romantic. By allowing yourself to bring this kind of mindset into your relationship, will not only help to strengthen the foundation of your union, it will bring more excitement into your lives. Plus, when you live and lose yourself in romantic times, you live free from the thought of boredom knocking on the door, walking in and ripping your affair into threads.

It's not that hard to live and think as a romantic. All you have to remember is that romance is a process that you make happen. How do you make it happen? You make it happen by being creative and clever. Start looking at your marriage as an opportunity to be expressive with your love. Allow the sky to be the limit with your imagination with soft music, lighting and candles.

Romantic Mornings:

Romantic mornings can get your day off to a delicious start. Set your alarm clock early enough to spend at least an hour or so together before heading off to work. Enjoy morning love and start the day with tons of energy. Share a light breakfast in bed after the lovemaking. Or better yet, throw on your robe and light a candle at the kitchen table. It doesn't matter what you're serving, whether it's French toast and hash browns or just a bowl of cereal. The idea is to sit there together and enjoy it. Sharing a meal right after lovemaking has a way of giving instant energy to a couple. Don't be surprised if you pay another visit to the bedroom before your two hours are up.

Romantic Calls:

There's nothing quite like the sound of your lover's voice when he's not around and you're thinking of him. The telephone is a lover's tool. It was made for lovers. It's at your fingertips 24 hours a day. Call when your lover is down and worried, to say good night, or to say good morning. Call to say "I love you." A phone call can be an instant electronic extension of romance, a way to be loving across a country, a mountain range, or a street. Call your mate up at work and tell him something sweet and sexy, especially when he's away on business. When he's traveling away from home, he'll fantasize about you even more, sleeping and waking up in a hotel room all alone. Call his hotel room at 6:00 a.m. and give him a wake-up call with a sexy tidbit. And considering how the average man thinks about sex almost six times an hour, it goes to reason that calling him up with a sexy tidbit about how much you miss him and look forward to seeing him will keep him looking forward to knocking on your door. And when he does, give him the most passion-filled kiss you can muster.

Romantic Dinners:

Have him come home to a romantic meal. Light the candles before he arrives and set the mood by dimming the lights and having his favorite music playing in the background. Use your best china even if you're only serving a grilled cheese sandwich and French fries. If you have as full a work schedule as he does, you won't always have the luxury of time or energy to prepare a full course candlelight dinner at your place, but keep romantic candles and light dinners on the agenda for those occasions when you do feel fully rested. During one of your romantic evenings while dining out together, add a little mystery to the setting. Use your imagination and hide a small gift somewhere on your body. Then say to your mate, "I've got something for you, and it's hidden on me somewhere! Find it and it's all yours!" Be creative and watch the flames of passion rise.

Romantic Massages:

Turn down the light to where it leaves the room with a romantic haze. Try listening to soothing music as you both try giving each other as much pleasure as humanly possible. Try to get the most out of your romantic massage. Your partner has to help you do this by teaching you how and where he or she likes to be touched or kissed. That places all the responsibility on the teacher—the person who's getting the pleasure—for getting the utmost pleasure. When it's your turn to teach, make believe you are a queen or a king and you want to deserve as much pleasure as possible. You can teach each other verbally and non-verbally. You can put your hands on his or hers to guide them, indicating where, how, and how much pressure.

Or simply tell your partner what you wish or guide your partner's head to where you'd like to be kissed. Always be aware of the warmth under your fingers and focus on whether the place you are touching is smooth, cool or rough. You might also focus on signs of pleasure in your partner, such as rapid breathing or subtle body movements. And remember, a massage, even an erotic massage, doesn't have to lead to anything other than what it is. A massage doesn't have to be some-thing you do on the way to something else, but rather for its own sake; for the pleasure it gives you and your man. In the spirit, outside the pressures of time and performance, try not to head in any one direc-tion, but explore where the mood and pleasures lead you.

Romantic Nights:

After a romantic night on the town dancing and dining, top the eve-ning off by giving him his favorite dessert; and then make the first move in bed. By making the first move, you will let him know that you are in the mood. Even if you're not used to it and feel somewhat uncomfortable with it, ease into it and give it a try. You will find that initiating lovemaking will make his heart pound for you! According to Dr. John Gray, author of *What Your Mother Couldn't Tell You & Your Father Didn't Know*, "if he is turned on for you and you appear not even to be interested in making love, it can be very embarrassing to him. Because when a man loves a woman, the most potent way he can feel her love is during lovemaking. During arousal a man is most sensitive to receiving and giving love; to be rejected when he is aroused is generally the most difficult challenge for him to handle in a relationship."

Chapter 4

17 Places to Meet Your Mate

Since the beginning of time, men and women have been looking for their soul mates—that one special person made just for them. Men and women will go to the ends of the earth looking for that one special person who will make their life complete! But to meet your dream man, first you have to find him; and to find him, you have to get out there and go places! For sure, the more people you meet, the more likely you are to find someone compatible. When you think about it, it's really not necessary for any of us to roam across the country to find that significant other. Statistics show that more than 50 percent of marriages in this country are between individuals who lived within a few miles of each other. The bottom line in meeting that special someone is to get out and meet people.

The mystical thing about meeting your soul mate is that you won't know what you will be doing or where you will be when that person pops into your world. You could be shopping for groceries, attending a wedding, or just walking your dog. But when it happens, there's usually an instant connection, you feel comfortable and at ease!

Weddings:

If you get an invitation to go to Kim's wedding, don't debate how you don't care for Kim. Just go! What better place to meet the man of your dreams than at a wedding? After all, love is in the air! The beautiful flowers and flowing champagne spells romance with a capital R! You're dressed to die for in your best clothing, and the man across the room looks quite handsome in his best suit. Think of the romantic background music and the dancing, and the time is perfect to meet your prince. The bride or groom usually knows the people they have invited, so they can easily introduce you to that one handsome fellow who catches your eye.

Laundromats:

It doesn't seem that romantic to meet someone while they are sorting their dirty laundry, but it seems to be a popular meeting place. Any day of the week, single men and women are popping in and out of Laundromats, now that they don't have their mothers to wash for them. You could meet your soul mate while waiting for your clothes to dry. You have to wash your clothing and he has to wash his, and sometimes there's a meeting of the minds during the rinse cycle.

Libraries:

Someone I know ended up meeting the person they married at the public library. They were both at the same table, at the same time, on the same day, looking for the same information, when their eyes met and they introduced themselves and exchanged phone numbers. If you are thinking that the library is the last place you would like to spend your time, think again about how many men and women frequent libraries. Visualize a quiet comfortable place to run into that special person. You look up and he's walking over to your table.

Romantic Cruises:

If you have always wanted to take a cruise, go for it. Taking one of those big ships across the vast waters could land you in the arms of your Prince Charming. Just imagine being on a beautiful cruise across blue waters that seem to have no beginning or end. While taking a moonlight stroll, enjoying the fresh night air, that special guy taps you on the shoulder. The two of you meet and end up watching the stars together.

Grocery Store:

Ask anybody and they would probably think of a grocery store as the most unlikely place to bump into any prince or princess. After all who is thinking of meeting someone while they're shopping for food. But it has happened. In fact, I know someone who it has happened to on several occasions. It could happen to you. Next time you go grocery shopping just make sure you're not wearing rollers in your hair.

Exercise Gym:

It's long been known that workout clubs are a great meeting spot to run into someone who is into the same thing you are—keeping fit. So, it might work in your benefit to become a regular at your local workout gym. Guys and girls come a dime-a-dozen at workout clubs, usually having regular workout schedules. So, any time of the week is a good time to go work out and possibly run into your soul mate.

Hardware Stores:

There may be something you could use from a hardware store. Try shopping there sometimes. Men flock to these stores all the time looking for nails and bolts to fix this and that. And chances are, if you bump into your soul mate at one of these stores, he will at least be handy around the house.

Volunteer Work:

Depending on the type of man you're looking to meet, volunteer at the place of your choice. If your heart is set on a television personality type, volunteer at one of your local TV stations; or volunteer at your nearest hospital, if your heart is set on a meeting a doctor or someone in the medical profession.

Comedy Clubs:

Everyone loves to laugh, and when you're laughing, you feel at ease. Comedy clubs usually bring out the smiles and laughter, so much so, in fact, that no ice-breakers are needed. You're all laughs and smiles.

Conversation will become easy if your Prince Charming happens to be seated next to you.

Picnics:

Picnics are fun and relaxing whether you go with family or friends or just take a blanket and a basket of food out to the park on your own. The fresh summer air is relaxing as you sit on your blanket enjoying your sandwich and chips. His blanket, where he's lying in the sun, could end up just yards from yours.

Video Store:

This is not to imply that men watch more movies than women, but whenever I go into one, there always seem to be more men in these video stores than women. Just like you, chances are he's there because he needs a movie to pass the time. Maybe you two could strike up a conversation and end up watching the movie together.

Hobby Shops:

Girls, you can shop at a man's hobby shop alone if you would like, but it may be best to go to one of these shops with your father or brother. This way you won't look too out of place while you browse hoping to spot that one special man.

Bowling Alleys:

Bowling is a very popular sport that attracts a lot of men and women. It's a very sociable setting and whether you know how to bowl or not, it's a fun place to go with friends and just hang out. Chances are, with all the men in attendance, one is sure to catch your eye.

Biking:

If you like biking, join a bike club. You're biking, he's biking. For starters, you both have that one thing in common. To break the ice, you could compliment his bike, and he'll probably compliment yours. Who knows, you could end up making a date to bike together.

Anniversary Celebrations:

An anniversary celebration offers a comfortable, romantic setting where the celebrated couple has invited family and friends and their friend's friends. You could meet a gorgeous step-cousin who could be all that you have been waiting for in a man.

Long Distance Train Rides:

On your next long distance trip, instead of using your frequent flyer miles, book a seat on the train. You two can share a seat together, share your meals and drinks together, and tell each other your life stories, while traveling to your destination.

Hotel Lounges:

If you're looking for the business or executive type, they hold meetings, do business, socialize and drink in hotel lounges seven days a week. You could meet prince charming here, but get ready for a long distance affair, if he's from out of town.

Many people feel—it really doesn't matter where you meet, as long as you meet! Here's to a happy meeting!

Chapter 5

6 Ways to Land Your Romeo by Playing Hard to Get

If you keep falling into the trap of meeting nice men, but watching each one wave good-bye for one reason or another, don't keep stacking up each experience as "his loss." If he is someone you want to be with it's your loss too. Look in the mirror and start with yourself. Do you stand strong or give in too easily? Not standing your ground and giving in too easy is one way to send him walking away from you. "I gave him everything and he still didn't love me, is a story I've heard over and over again from women."

There are several reasons why we women feel we have to give everything. We've been brought up by a generation of mothers who gave their all to our fathers. We've been taught to be the nurturers of society, the nurses, the teachers, the caretakers. Besides, if we give everything, we think the man will take care of us.

Men, on the other hand, are taught that they have to work hard for what they get. Men go out into the world and do battle on a daily basis. They enjoy the fight of working hard for something and then achieving that goal. So the problem with giving a man everything in the beginning of a relationship is that he doesn't have anything to work for, to achieve. That doesn't mean that you can't go out with a man, make love with him, even live with him—but there must be something more he'll get if he marries you or makes a commitment to you. Otherwise, what's his motivation? There's no challenge.

A story about a woman named Helen: Helen, a successful motion picture studio executive, was a woman who had everything. At only thirty-four she had already acquired a house in the hills with a swimming pool and a great view of Los Angeles. Her house was filled with artwork and fine furniture. She traveled around the world and could afford the best clothes and the fanciest cars—all of which she had. But Helen didn't have a committed relationship and she was really unhappy about the lack of love in her life. "I don't understand why some guy doesn't jump at the chance of a relationship with me," she bemoaned her single fate. "I have so much to offer." Helen said.

Helen was suffering from a severe case of "good girl" syndrome. While living a modern and sophisticated big-city life, she was also trying to be the perfect traditional "good girl." To Helen, being a perfect "good girl" meant that she could only be a lover of one man at a time. Being a good girl also meant that she had to try for a "falling in love" relationship with every man she went to bed with. After all, she thought, good girls only go to bed with a man they're serious about. In order to see herself as a good girl, to justify the sex she wanted. Helen always gave too much too soon. She cooked gourmet dinners for the man she dated, bought him clothes, made plans, bought theater tickets and was always available. No matter how unfulfilling the relationship, Helen had to be faithful. Frantically she worked at showing each man what a perfect wife she would be.

The men Helen dated were scared off without her understanding why. After a few dates, just as a man was getting seriously interested in his pursuit of Helen, the pursuit was suddenly over, consummated. Helen would be his—body and soul, and heart. She was ready to give her all, the way a good girl does. Only that was more than the man had bargained for—at least at that stage of their relationship. Helen failed to understand that, despite her good intentions, her rush to commit her love could turn an intriguing affair into a heavy, almost threatening, situation for the man. Men generally have two reactions to this situation. Some will take advantage of the sex and the other offerings while being extra careful not to "get in too deep." The relationship has nowhere to go, the guy soon gets bored, and he moves on. The other reaction is for a man to really worry about why so much is being offered so soon, chalk it up to extreme neediness, and leave immediately.

By offering everything too soon, Helen seemed needy. There's nothing that will turn a healthy man off faster than a really needy woman. The worst impression you can give a man is that there is nobody else in your life. Men are competitive by nature. If he can't compete for you, he's likely to find a more challenging woman, one he'll have to fight for.

That's what kept happening to Helen. Her relationships never lasted more than six months. By the time six months were over, the man had more of Helen than he ever wanted, and he was off looking for someone a little harder to get. Remember the old adage, "Play hard to get." It's partially true. Only instead of playing hard to get you should be hard to get. Practice turning him down.

1.   The next time he asks you out, tell him you'd love to see him but you already have plans. That's what you'd do if you really are busy and not too eager. And that's what will perk his interest. A man wants a woman who is popular and hard to get. He wants to feel he has a prize other men want—not someone nobody cares about.

2.   See more than one man, especially if you're interested in a serious relationship. If there is one special man you are interested in, you will need to have lots of men in your life, just to keep Mr. Right's attention. You don't have to go to bed with them all if you don't want to; he'll think you did anyway. "Then the man I want won't have any respect for me," Helen worried when I told her she had

to diversify. "He'll think I'm loose and easy," Helen thought. "Soon Helen began to realize that in truth she had been too easy all along, that she actually gave too much for too little. Finally she decided to take matters into her own hands. She joined a dating service. She couldn't believe the change in the men she knew. The minute her current, couldn't-care-less lover found out Helen was coming to the attention of thousands of eligible men, he became suddenly very attentive. By then, Helen realized she didn't want him. She was already dating lots of other men—and starting out on the right foot in her new relationships.

3. You must use self-control on your urges to give. Set up a situation where the man has to do something to get you—not where you work hard to get him. The relationship must have somewhere to go; you must give it time to develop.

4. Never overwhelm a man by giving too much too soon, because that's psychologically bad for the future success of your relationship. Perhaps the hardest thing is to do nothing in a relationship, but often it's the only sound thing to do. The best way to keep a man coming back is to dole out little bits of you at a time, just enough to keep him interested but not too much. Always leave him wanting more of you—not relieved that you're gone.

5. There are very sound psychological principles behind returning a man's affection less than totally—especially in the beginning of a relationship. Being rewarded once in a while, somewhat unpredictably, makes men and women work harder to achieve a prize. If you're clever, you can use this information to make a man really want you, and work hard to win you.

6. Sit back, relax. Let him come to you. He will, because you know the secrets of reaching out to him without seeming needy.

It takes self-control to keep from throwing yourself at a man when you spot Mr. Right. If you feel tempted to do the wrong thing, to call him on a made-up excuse, he'll see right through it. Develop an understanding with a friend who will be supportive. Use the buddy system and call your friend when you feel tempted to blow it with a man you're interested in. The phone is so easy. His number keeps going through your head. You must resist! One phone call too many or one winsome gift too many can ruin everything you've worked hard to establish. Breaking old habits isn't easy, but when they're bad love habits, breaking them can be more than worthwhile. If you've had trouble with relationships, learning not to give too much too soon can mean the difference between success and failure.

When he gives his all, you give yours. If he has made a commitment and you have too, if you've mutually decided this is it, if you've become an exclusive couple, then you should be almost totally giving.

No matter how much you give, there will always be a private part of you that's just you, your core. That's the part you can never give away. It may be just ten percent, but it's you. Treasure it.

Chapter 6

Meet and Marry a Rich Prince

Being in a relationship with that one special guy and sharing a life together is what most women dream about and look forward to. We all want to meet our prince charming who will make our hearts tingle. And as a female, we possess something quite unique, which is the ability to be able to get a man at the drop of a hat. But having that great quality isn't enough to land us a rich husband. It takes something more: The know-how! And why not seek to fall in love with a rich guy? It's just as easy to fall in love with a rich man as it is a poor one. But the problem with falling in love with a rich man—you got to meet him first.

I heard a wise woman once say, "You can dig in a trash can all day and all you're going to pull out is garbage!" In other words, don't expect to meet an oil tycoon or a big time lawyer sitting at the table next to you at the corner bar and grill, or sharing your shopping aisle at your local shopping mall. It can happen, but most likely it won't. Because—think about it—why should he? He can afford to shop and eat anywhere. Think about it before you start having negative thoughts—thinking to yourself, "If where I shop and eat isn't good enough for him, then he's not good enough for me, and he can stay on his high horse and keep trucking!" Ask yourself, would you settle for a $7 steak if you could afford to pay $20?

The First Rule—He's Not Better than You:

The most important rule in meeting a wealthy man is to not fall into a trap of thinking that the rich man thinks he's better than you, because if you think that way and he senses that you feel that way, your affair will be doomed from the start and will never get off the ground! It will never work!

The Second Rule—Go Where He Is:

The second rule in meeting and possibly marrying your rich prince is to go where he is. Put yourself in his circle. His circle being where he works, where he eats, where he shops, where he goes for entertainment.

The Third Rule—Have Confidence in Yourself:

The third rule is to have enough confidence in yourself to know that after you meet this man that you are worth his efforts. Push away little nagging thoughts in the back of your mind that ask "what can I offer this man? He has everything." Just bear in mind that he only wants from you what you want from him—Love. According to Ann Landers in her book, *Wake Up and Smell the Coffee*, "If you have love in your life, it can make up for a great many things you lack. If you don't have it, no matter what else there is, it's not enough." So just remember—you have plenty to give when you have your love to offer.

The Fourth Rule—Get Him to Notice You:

Have the class and the look to get him to notice you once you do bump into him. Men are visual individuals. They are excited by what they see. Usually from the moment he spots you, he knows if he likes what he sees. And it's not that you have to look like a beauty queen, but there has to be something about your physical appearance that attracts him to you. It could be your smile, your hair, your figure or your legs. So take a great effort in making sure you're well groomed from your neat hair style to your neat manicure, right down to your stylish new shoes. Look the look, walk the walk, and talk the talk; and that rich husband will be yours for the asking! Now you may be asking yourself, do you have the class to snag a rich man? According to Ann Landers, "Class never runs scared. It is surefooted and confident and it can handle whatever comes along. Class bespeaks an aristocracy unrelated to ancestors or money. A blue blood can be totally without class while the son of a Welsh miner may ooze class from every pore. Everyone is comfortable with the person who has class because he is comfortable with himself."

Have you ever wondered why the rich marry rich? For example: Movie stars marry movie stars. Television personalities marry other television personalities. It's quite simple. People get involved with and marry persons they work with or meet where they work, which brings us back to the second rule.

Where He Works:
Let's say you have your heart set on falling in love with and possibly marrying a doctor, one suggestion would be to get a job at your local hospital. And if you don't have any qualifying skills for the administrative, executive or medical positions, take a job in the cafeteria. Yes, the lunch room! You're not looking for a lifetime career serving soup. You're just trying to catch a rich husband. But if there's nothing available in the cafeteria, your last option would be to sign up as a volunteer. Hospitals always need volunteers

Where He Parties:
The rich like to party and dance as much as anyone else, and since you like going to dances and parties anyway, and sometimes you will drive miles to get to one, why not put forth a little effort and seek out the ones where you know the big wigs will be.

Where He Hangs Out:
Many of the fancy hotels cater to the wealthy executive types: vice-presidents, directors, CEO's, heads of corporations and pilots—just to name a few. Any night of the week, and sometimes on weekends, you will find the lounges of most fine hotels crawling with wealthy businessmen. But bear in mind, most of these men who frequent the hotel's lounges are doing so because they probably have a room there

and will only be in town for a few days, and, even worse, some of them could be married. But, most likely, some will also be single.

If you're wondering how to get a chance to rub shoulders with these big executive types, it's simple. Just make plans to spend an evening at one of the most exclusive hotels in town, and you don't have to rent a room. Just take your briefcase and a note pad, and of course be dressed like a business type if possible and sit there in the lounge with your briefcase and note pad on the table. Never approach any of the guys! And try not to look around the room too much. You don't want to appear desperate and out of place. Just sit there as if you could care less while sipping on a diet soda or spring water.

If you're thinking, what if you sit there all evening and still don't get noticed or asked out by one of those big wigs? It's possible that you won't get asked out, but the bottom line is you are putting yourself right in the middle of his hang out, and that increases the chances that you could get asked out!

Where He Eats:
Many fine restaurants have a bar section, where they serve cocktails and sometimes have live bands. That's the section you want to head to if you're dining alone. Sit there in the bar section and order your meal or sip on your drink and watch all the rich single men walk in. Some will have dates on their arms, but some of them will not, and who knows one might just sit next to you at the bar.

The idea is to frequent the places rich men frequent and before you know it, that special one could ask you out. From there the two of you could develop a beautiful relationship and get married. You will have the man of your dreams! And he's rich to boot!

Chapter 7

The Big 10: Men Who Are Losers

We don't always register the signs men give off about their nature or about what they will be like as partners. We don't always pick the kinds of men we end up with—we are often on the receiving end. We also do not love men "too much" in a vacuum; some of them compel us to love them that way. Many men know how to hold a woman in an emotional vortex and succeed very well in doing so. Nor can we necessarily alter our choices in men or unions—especially merely by changing ourselves. We often don't have the opportunity. Moreover, we make some of our choices on purpose, knowing the problems we are getting into, and are content with them.

If you've had a few unsuccessful relationships with men who treat you badly, chances are, you were hooked up with one of the "Big 10 Losers." If you've had a lot of these experiences, you may be really stuck in the "Loser Trap." You may be a bit cynical. You may feel that all men are losers, but that just is not so. If you've had an unbroken string of losers, now is the time to take stock. You may have a fatal fascination for losers. You may not really be ready for a committed relationship. You may be picking the wrong men or you may be teaching perfectly okay men to act like losers—without even knowing you're doing it.

29

According to Dr. Tracy Cabot, author of *How to Make a Man Fall In Love With You*, the "Loser Trap" is one of the hardest to break out of. The first step is to admit to yourself that there are nice guys out there—guys who are open to and capable of giving real love. You don't have to pick ready-made losers if you can spot them ahead of time. We all get involved with at least one loser in our life time. We may marry him, live with him, or just go with the jerk. Ask any female who has been involved with a loser and you'll find that they all seem to have one thing in common—they all say they didn't know he was like that. [He was so nice in the beginning].

The Big 10: The Loser Checklist

1. The Ladies' Man:
This guy loves women, lots of women and thinks about them all the time. He looks at every pretty face he sees. If he could live his fantasy, it would be to have several females between his sheets at the same time. He knows he wants that, but he's not keen on any other decision; so don't expect him to make a decision. He won't make a decision. He's not sure of anything, including whether he wants you. One reason he can't decide is because he's greedy. He really wants everything. He's afraid he's missing something with someone else each minute he's with you. Ever wondered why he never makes a date ahead of time? He's afraid something better might come along at the last minute, and then he'd be committed to you and unhappy all night thinking about what he might have missed. He breaks dates often, especially after the initial glow of a relationship is fading. You always know it's because he thinks he might get something better. He never stops looking, even after he's been married for years.

There's no real fun in a relationship with a lady's man because he's never satisfied with anything. He can't enjoy the "here and now" because he's always imagining a prettier face and a trimmer body. No real woman ever lives up to the fantasy one in his head.

The ladies' man is also the kind of man who can change his attitude about life in the blink of an eye. He might consider changing his address or career in a matter of minutes. Nothing he already has is ever any good for very long. He thinks that more, or different, or new acquisitions will make him happy. What he really needs is a good therapist and not a woman.

2. The Control Freak:

He is a natural critic and speaks only from his own perfection. He works, but usually in a position where he makes good money, doing rarely anything, preferring to tell other people what to do. When you meet him, he immediately gives you all his credits, and lets you know you're very lucky he's chosen you. Naturally, you're impressed by his good taste. It's obvious from the way he criticizes everyone else that you're the perfect two. If it isn't obvious, he tells you. He knows how you should dress, put your makeup on, even wear your hair, and as long as you agree, he's happy.

He knows what will make you happy too. He will direct your career, tell you how to talk to your mother, even what you want in lovemaking. He knows without a doubt that what you really need most is him. And since he's all you need, why do you need to call up your girlfriend or spend any time with anyone else who may happen to want some of your time, like your sister.

There's always a moment when things start to go sour in a relationship with a control freak: when he discovers you don't dust the tops of the doors. The first chink in your perfection is his opening. From there he splits your self-confidence apart, leaving your ego in little pieces. Suddenly, you can't do simple things you always did almost automatically. If you make coffee, the pot burns up. If it's a roast, it's still frozen on the inside. There's no way you can do anything right. It's all down from there. Soon the slightest infraction of the control freak's rules of conduct turns him into a raging beast and you into a tear-dripping mess.

Strong defiance is the best way to get rid of a control freak. Wear the red dress he hates. Don't tell your best friend you can't talk on the phone when he's there. Make plans with friends he doesn't like.

3. The Bad Boy:
Somehow this bad news loser makes you yearn to be taken into his confidence. You can't wait to know all about his shady friends. It's clear that when he admits his criminal dealings to you, you should be flattered. You've earned his sacred trust.

The next step after trust is involvement. He even offers you a profit. All you have to do is let him leave 300 pounds of marijuana in your attic for a couple of weeks. Or go on a stolen credit card shopping spree with him. You're perfectly safe, he insists. And even if you don't get arrested, you soon find that your nerves aren't holding you together the way they used to—before you met him. And maybe you're nervous because be showed you all his scars and broken bones, or he brought a gun to your apartment, or you think your phone is being tapped by the CIA, or that you're still shaking after your first date.

If you hang in—for the excitement, the sex, or whatever—it gets worse. Soon he starts treating you like his property. You and whatever you own are now his possessions. The easiest way to get rid of him is to admit you think the police are watching your house.

4. The Sex Fiend:
This type is actually out for one thing and we all know what it is. He was born this way and he'll never change. He can be any guy. The guy next door to the mailman, but all he wants is sex from you. Commitment is not in his vocabulary. Long-term relationship is not in his vocabulary. He's just looking for a good time with whoever will give it to him. It's hard to spot a sex fiend because they are so smooth, saying all the right words and making all the right moves. You'll never know you have been had, until you have been had. You wake up with an empty feeling in your stomach after a magical night of romance and you know deep down that he's history—on to his next prey. You may ask yourself "can you win this type over to marriage?" Maybe, but his

bottom line is still the same. He's a sex fiend, remember? And a sex fiend can't change his spots even if he wanted to. It's in his blood. He's not about to settle for sex from one female for the rest of his life. You can play hard to get, and he'll marry you just to get you in his bed. But after the honeymoon, he's out on the hunt, having affairs behind your back.

5. The Achiever:

The achiever is a successful, financially secure man who's dedicated to his work. He is an admirable member of society but a lousy partner in a relationship. He pays little attention to you and is often too tired to do anything but sleep when he takes time off. Your love for each other is a grain of sand compared to the global grandeur of his more time-consuming passion. But he does have some advantages. He is dependable for some things. He always knows what time it is, he makes dates well in advance, and if he can't show, he'll either call or be apologetic.

It's easy to get sucked in by an achiever. On the surface he's such a good citizen, hard working, affluent, even intelligent. He's the man your mother always dreamed you'd marry. So, it's impossible not to think of marriage with him, because an achiever offers financial security and obviously needs a wife. Then he could devote more time to his work without having to worry about details like cooking or cleaning house. "Actually, a robot would do if she looked good. If you try to get him away from his work, he will only make you feel tacky and small. If all this upsets you, don't complain to your mother or friends; they'll agree with him."

The achiever is universally admired, but when it comes to returning love, he's a loser. If you don't want to spend your life lonely and miserable, don't even start to get involved with this guy.

6. The Player:

Remember the saying, everybody plays a fool? That's what the player banks on, you being a fool, so he can play you. Once you come face to face with a player and get involved in his game, you'll always be able to spot one.

Leisurely time spent with this man just doesn't happen. He doesn't have any. He always falls asleep immediately after making love, if he doesn't fall asleep without making love. Don't worry about making breakfast in the morning, because he's already gone.

7. The Cripple:
This guy is one you can't help but feel sorry for. This guy is in a lot of pain. He needs a friend more than anything else. He is still wounded from a recent break-up with his girl friend or ex-wife. He's an emotional basket case. He usually lives alone.

The cripple will probably get better, but it may take years. It's certain that you don't want to be the first woman he gets involved with after his divorce. He's still bleeding and too involved with his own pain and losses to make a good mate for you. He's worried about his ex-wife. The guy she's sleeping with, what her lawyer's taking away from him, the house he already lost, the kids he doesn't know whether he'll be able to keep seeing. How he's going to make alimony and child support payments? She took something of his that he wants back. And he wants his things back more than he wants a relationship with you or anyone else.

Sex with a cripple is usually a disaster since nothing about his body seems to operate or function probably. If it does, he feels guilty right afterward. The way to get rid of the cripple is to refuse to listen to any more stories about his ex-wife, his divorce, what he lost, his kids, or his past. Refuse to sympathize. Tell him you think his ex was a very lovely person.

8. The Time Bomb:
The time bomb is your classic unstable personality hidden behind the face of an average looking guy. Time bombs come in several varieties—latent alcoholics, compulsive gamblers, obsessive Don Juans, drug abusers, physical abusers, and just plain crazies. If you could see the inner person, you wouldn't go near him. The problem is that the time bomb seems normal on the surface, and it's hard to hear the time bomb ticking.

He's so nice in the beginning that you tend to get hooked. Then, just as you begin to feel certain that true love has at last felled you and someone else at the same time, an explosion invariably rocks your security with a time bomb. And, of course the first time it happens, you don't recognize it as a pattern.

Afterwards, he swears he is reformed; he'll never binge, gamble, cheat, hit you, or go crazy again. If he's got you hooked, you keep loving him. You forgive him, and soon the two of you are together again. But the signs were there all along. His ex-wife doesn't speak to him, his former live-in girl friend is in an institution for the mentally disturbed, and a jealous male or female is always trying to get him. He hates his job whatever it is. And "If you listen closely, he'll give you clues. A time bomb seems to enjoy telling about his perilous personal life: how his ex-wife tried to run him over with her car, how some guy tried to shoot him for dating his girl."

The temptation to hang around and wait for your beautiful romance to bloom once more can be seductive, but the time bomb is seriously disturbed, almost always self-destructive, and sometimes very dangerous. If you've got a time bomb in your life, accept that his life pattern is unchangeable. Divide up your possessions and separate your bank accounts first. Then change your phone number and the locks on your door.

9. The Gigolo:

This type allows women to house and feed him. They go through jobs like women. If he wasn't working when you met him, don't expect him to find a job just because he's shacking up with you. The gigolo is the type of guy who doesn't believe in working for too long of a time for anybody.

The gigolo is easy to spot because he's cute as a picture and can charm the skin off of a snake. He arrives at your house and just stays. He doesn't have to call home because he doesn't have one. He is always broke and hungry when he gets to your house and will stay as long as you feed him and give him lots of love. He's sweet and helpful around the house and a wonderful lover. He has a way of just fitting in. But when he finishes with lovemaking he usually finds something urgent he must do. He never takes you anywhere. He's either about to make a fortune or has just lost one. He expects to be nurtured between fortunes.

No matter how much you give the gigolo, he doesn't give anything back, except playing the guitar and making love. When he's around, he's romantic and attentive, and you miss both when he's gone, but he's really a bad bet for a long-term relationship. And you can get rid of the gigolo easily enough by either cutting off his support system or asking for a month's contribution to food and rent in advance.

10. The Patient:

The patient really wants you to take care of him. His mother wasn't very warm or loving and he is still looking for the woman who will make up for her inadequacies. There is nothing he won't do to exploit your motherly side.

He's just your basic sympathy sponge. Patients have been known to fake illness so well that they really make themselves sick. You are supposed to stand by, ever ready to hold his hand at the crucial moment. There's no limit to the illnesses he can conjure up or inflict on himself. "You can guarantee the patient will have an abominable toothache in the middle of your birthday party. It seems as if you're always rushing him to an emergency room. Each new catastrophe requires a new, healthy diet, different vitamins, and the most sincere concern for the funnel functions of his body. Patients make so much noise when they have an orgasm you think they're going to die." And afterward, instead of tender words from him you get deep rasping noises as he flings himself across the bed and clutches his chest. You always pray he doesn't die on top of you.

You can discourage the Patient by hiding all the medications in your house, even aspirin. Tell him you're a believer in faith healing and that if he wants to get well his mind will cure him. The next time you hear his agonized yell of pain, say you'll be there when you finish meditating. Complain of various lurid female problems that you think might be contagious.

Men who've gotten away with treating women badly for a long time just can't help trying the same thing with you. You might be able to make him treat you differently, but only if you put your foot down the very first time he does anything out of line. The point is, you can't let a loser get away with anything, not even once, or you're in trouble!

Chapter 8

8 Simple Steps to Ask Him Out for a Date

Sometimes all it takes is one simple hello or one friendly smile. For some of us, the hardest thing to do is to let a man we are attracted to know that we are attracted to him. No doubt it has happened to every female at one point or another. You were probably at a party, out dancing, at church, buying groceries, at the Laundromat, at school or work and you have laid eyes on the most appealing man that you wanted to meet. You froze up, afraid the sky would come tumbling down or the world would stop spinning if you even attempted to approach him. You missed the chance to meet him, because you didn't have the courage to make the first move. Don't repeat the cycle. Take charge of what you want and muster up the nerve to ask him out.

He's someone you would definitely like to meet and maybe get to know better. You're hoping he'll notice you and want to approach you, but the clock is ticking and you're getting anxious. He hasn't really noticed you, or paid much attention to your noticing him. So he doesn't seem to be coming your way and you don't want him to get away. You don't want to miss the opportunity of meeting him and finding out if he's someone you would like to get to know better. So now you want to approach him and, maybe muster up the nerve to ask him out, but you're not sure how.

- Look at him until his eyes meet yours. Once he spots you, make sure you give him a friendly smile. Don't try to give him a sexy look—just be yourself. A guy can see right through phoniness and that will turn him off.

- If he just looks and smiles back at you without attempting to approach you, don't let what appears to be a lack of interest on his part discourage your efforts. Now it's your turn to muster your courage and approach him. Ask any guy and most of them will agree, that nothing flatters a man more than having a female approach him. Remember that most men are very much afraid of rejection and many will sit or stand against the wall and look at women. By approaching him, you will give him all the courage he needs.

- Walk up to him and say, "Hi." Break the ice by looking about the surroundings and make a comment about where you are. "This place is crowded," "The music here is great," "Do you come here often?"

- In whatever you say or do, make sure you don't appear nervous. Don't just be in charge. Act in charge. Hold your head up and look directly at him.

- Now all you have to do is just smile and stay by his side. He will probably be so flattered, that he'll take the initiative and ask you out.

- After giving him about twenty minutes or so of your time and he hasn't shown that much interest or hasn't asked for your number, and he just seems indifferent about your company, now is the time for you to ask him out. (If you feel you would really like to see him again or get to know him better). The best way to ask him out is to just mention some upcoming event you know of. Ask him if he would like to accompany you. My money is on him. I bet he'll be more than pleased to do so.

■ You have asked him out, and if he says he has plans for the particular time in question, and offers no rain check or suggestion for future get together, he's rejecting your offer. When that happens, keep your chin up and discreetly make yourself scarce from his company; it's his loss.

■ No one likes rejection, but when you take the initiative, you're setting yourself up for rejection, as well as acceptance. But do not let it hinder you. You gave it your best shot. Now you don't have to waste any more time in the company of someone who isn't interested. You can now mingle and put forth your efforts toward another potential future date.

Now that you know how to get his attention, you don't have to sit at home alone and wait for some guy to ask you out. Go get him! Get out there and ask him out. And you will have success; but if you don't, just remember, you tried and it's not your loss, it's his. At least you'll know you can do it. Plus, there's always a next time! So here's to happy dating!

Chapter 9

5 Reasons Why Smart Women Love Stupid Jerks

We are intelligent! We are clever! We are one hundred and one beautiful things and more! We can run two companies at once while juggling night classes, three children and two pets. We are not mind readers. We can't see inside of a man's brain. We don't have a built-in radar that lets us know when a jerk is coming our way. In a perfect world, jerks would have signs on their heads which read "Jerk: Take your Chances," but as things are, we have no foolproof way to spot one in advance and protect ourselves from him.

Intelligent women, it seems, are always falling prey to jerks. Why? Because we allow our hearts to control us. So regardless of how smart, strong or pretty we are, we do things for our men and accept behavior that we never thought we would tolerate.

The jerk is "always charming in the beginning," and that's what gets you interested. But, he soon "starts trying to see how much he can get away with. And poor you, you're so in love with his good side that you begin to put up with his bad side.

As a result, we allow our hearts to accept what in any other setting would be deemed inappropriate behavior. Lateness, poor excuses and absences. If he were a business partner, an employee, or just a platonic friend, you would tell him about himself or would just cut him off. But now your heart is involved and you just don't know how to handle him. And as the saying goes, "Men will only do what you allow them to," so the situation never improves.

Have you ever found yourself paired up with a jerk? If so, welcome to life! You have nothing to be ashamed of. We're all human and sometimes we make mistakes, but the million-dollar question is: "Why do smart, intelligent women stay with jerks?"

You Need Someone to Blame:
Living with a jerk allows you to blame your man for your problems. If you are this woman, you are obviously having difficulties addressing your own problems. And your man is the least of them. In fact, if it wasn't your man, it would be something or someone else.

Low Self-Esteem:
Low self-esteem can make it difficult for you to stand up for yourself and take charge of your life. "Low self-esteem may lead a woman to feel that she deserves no better than a lousy guy. She may also be trying to find self worth in her attachment to a particular man. Some men are drawn to women who are needy in that sense. It makes it easier for them to control and manipulate the relationship.

Repeated Family Pattern:
We stay with jerks because we are unconsciously falling into a family pattern. What type of man did your mother marry? If she was a single parent, what type of men did she expose you to? What was her attitude about men. Did she think having any man was better than none at all? The answer to any or all of these questions could shed light on your approach to relationships.

Other Subconscious Factors:
Are you subconsciously thinking, if I can reform him, it will be like reforming the father that my mother couldn't. "Few of us evaluate a prospective partner with the same objectivity and clarity that we might use to select a household appliance or a car," says. "Too many

unconscious factors get in the way." She explains that one of the most powerful influences on our choice of a mate is our experience in our first family—including the quality of our parents' relationships to each other, to us, and to their own family of origin."

Devalued Status of Singlehood:
If a woman doesn't have a man, society tells us, something must be wrong with us. As ridiculous and demeaning as this should sound, many of us believe it and choose to stay with jerks so that we don't have to be alone.

4 Women Explain Why They Stayed With Jerks:

Saving Face:
Karen, a bank executive says that she stayed with her jerk to save face. "My ex-husband Wesley was a big drinker and into drugs. I found all of this out about three months into our eight month marriage. We had only dated two months before I made the dreaded mistake of talking him into marrying me. After only three weeks into the marriage, he quit his job and began borrowing money from me. When I stopped lending, he started stealing out of the house. He couldn't help out with bills, but he was giving gifts to Liz, my 18-year-old daughter.

Did I kick him out after he started stealing from me?" She shakes her head. "No, I still stayed with the jerk. To leave him, I would have to admit I was a fool to force him into a marriage that he wasn't ready for—just so I could be able to say I was a Mrs. Eventually, Wesley left me. Liz left with him."

Weighty Issues:
Jacqueline, a 43-year-old schoolteacher, didn't dump her man because she was afraid of being lonely. "In 1983, when Paul and I met, I weighed about 125 lbs. At 5 feet I wasn't fat, but I weighed more than I wanted to, so I dieted to keep my weight under control. A few months after I married Paul, I got pregnant and my weight jumped an extra 50 pounds. After Latissa was born, I couldn't lose the weight. Paul started picking on me and treating me like he couldn't stand me.

He stopped touching me and never hugged me. He told me I was fat and ugly. He wouldn't take me anywhere. He said that I was too fat to be seen with him.

He said that if I left him, no other man would want me. I stayed with this guy because I was afraid of being alone. I was so afraid that what Paul said about my chances of getting another man was right. I took all kinds of abuse from him because I was more afraid of being alone than I was of being mistreated. In 1993, I finally got the nerve to leave him. I took Latissa and moved back to Chicago. I'm still having problems with my weight, but I have the love of my family and my daughter. I'm better off being single than being with some jerk who mistreats me.

Blind-Sided:
Louise, a 34-year-old attorney, says she stayed with the wrong man because she was deceived. "Sammy conned me. He knew just how to get what he wanted out of me. He used me for my money and education to help him get his big acting break.

I was home from California, visiting my parents, when I met him at my little brother's birthday party. He seemed fascinated with my life, with the fact that I was an attorney and doing okay for myself. After I went back home, we kept in touch, writing and calling each other, and within a year, he moved out to LA to live with me. I helped him get his acting career off the ground, and I didn't mind that he couldn't give me any financial support because he constantly made me feel loved and wanted. But when he got his first big acting part," she pauses, "he came clean. I mentioned marriage, and he admitted that he was still in love with his old girlfriend back home. His plan was to go be with her."

Cape Fear:
Sharlene, a 27-year-old waitress, says she was afraid to leave her man. "I know there are some good men out there. I just haven't had the luck of running into one. Ever since I can remember, I have always found myself in some dead-end relationship with some jerk. When

Chad and I started seeing each other, I felt he was different. He wanted something and was doing well for himself. We fell for each other, even though our jobs and education were miles apart, not to mention the 20-year difference in our ages. My family didn't care for him. They called him arrogant and self-centered and said he was too old for me. But what counted was that he was good to me.

After dating for four months, he asked me to move in with him. He couldn't give me enough. He was the first man to ever shower me with nice clothes and fine jewelry. But after I gave up my job, my apartment and all my friends for him, he showed me his other side, his abusive side. He became mentally and physically abusive, making me his puppet. After the first time he choked me, I was finally able to get away, but I stayed on as long as I did out of fear that he would harm me if I attempted to him leave."

Chapter 10

14 Dating Blunders to Avoid

Most of us have the best intentions at the beginning of a new relationship, then out of the blue before it gets off the ground, it is history. Something went wrong, but what? A dating mishap occurred that could have been prevented. Yes, we can prevent destroying a relationship by avoiding a few dating blunders.

Desperation!

The word desperation should be at the top of your list. It's the number one blunder to avoid. Under no circumstances should you allow someone to know that you are down-right desperate. You may know you're desperate, but no one else has to know. Avoid doing things that make you appear desperate, like going to a bar solely to find a relationship. You sound desperate when you go on and on about not having a man in your life. Men and women are like blood hounds when it comes to sensing a desperate man or woman. They are thinking, if you are so desperate to have someone in your life, then what's wrong with you? If something is wrong with you, I sure don't want to get hooked up with you.

Letting Looks Rule:

In many cases, when it comes to spotting that special someone across a room or across anywhere, looks usually rule. No matter who we are, we usually want someone in our lives who is at least halfway decent to look at. But then, there are those of us who go overboard and won't even give a halfway decent looking person the time of day. Their hair is not perfect, their clothes are not perfect, their eyes are not perfect. Something is not perfect, so you won't give the person a chance. The point is to stop focusing so much on good looks and give the person who just asked you to dance a chance. Who knows, they might have a lot more going for themselves than just their not-so-perfect-looks.

Being Thoughtless:

If you're out on a date with someone for the first time, if you think too much of yourself and talk too much about yourself, your date might find out more about you then he bargained for. Of course, you won't know a thing about him because he never got a chance to speak. Will he ask you out again? Who knows, he didn't get a word in edge-wise to ask you. The point here is don't make the big blunder of talking too much about yourself and what's going on in your life without giving your date a chance or opportunity to do the same.

Feeling Sorry for You:

When you feel sorry for yourself and feel like you don't have a friend in the world, even if these are your private thoughts, somehow you're going to attract everyone who agrees with your dim assessment of yourself. The key is to pick yourself up and feel like you are deserving of the world. That's who you will attract.

Sex Too Soon:

No one can tell the next adult when and how to engage in a sexual act. Most people have their own sexual code, and they are entitled to it. But it makes good sense to be acquainted with reality when it comes to something so personal as a complete giving of yourself. One reason not to sleep with someone without first developing an emotional bond is that a lot of us are a lot less ready than we think. Because reality is a hard punch in the stomach when your first time with your date ends up being your last. You get the point here.

Saying You'll Call:

This is a huge blunder that men and women make over and over again. If you went out with this person and you didn't enjoy the date and have no intentions of going out with that person again, don't promise you'll call and don't say it's okay for that person to call you. Be on the level by saying, I'm sorry, but I don't think it's going to work out. Nice knowing you. If you go the other route, he or she will keep calling you until you want to pull your hair out. They won't go away because they think you want them to call.

Creating Intimacy:

Be careful not to make the blunder of giving too much of yourself too soon. Your very private thoughts are a part of you and shouldn't be something that you can easily share with just anyone. If you're on any early date with someone you barely know and you share your most private self with him, he might make the following connection: He is a total stranger to you, and therefore your most private self is available to total strangers, and therefore you will have no intimacy left to make him feel like he's the special one whom you have chosen to trust. So he probably will not ask you out again. It's best to lay your cards on the table slowly.

Honesty Works:

Lying to someone who you hope to develop a love relationship with is absolutely a stupid thing to do. Don't make a huge blunder of telling your new date that you work as an executive if you really work as a waitress, or that you drive a Jaguar if you really drive a Honda. Because if you end up an item, he'll find out the truth anyway. Just be on the level about yourself. Honesty works. There's something warm and beautiful about listening to someone tell the truth, especially if it's a truth that puts them in a not-so-pleasing light.

Beating a Dead Horse:

You are beating a dead horse and making a big blunder when you are dating someone that you know is not right for you. How do you know they are not right for you? Because they have a trait that totally rips at you and keeps you down-hearted. You are sad more than you are happy; you are complaining more than you are smiling. And despite reasonable efforts on both your parts to work through the problems, the two of you just cannot get along. Stop beating a dead horse and move on. Realize that you cannot mold the man you're with into the perfect man that you want him to be.

Your Time With Him:

This blunder has caused many relationships to crumble. The blunder of asking the person you are married to or dating to give up their friends and family to spend more time with you. It's the most selfish, self-centered thing a mate can do to the other; especially when they say "if you don't spend every minute with me, then you don't love me." Spend time with him—but not so much that your life outside of him fades and dies.

Marriage Can't Fix It:

If you are dating and the problems overshadow the good times, don't make the blunder by jumping into a marriage thinking it will fix all. Because if you think you have problems now, just wait until you're married with two or more kids. So, if you're considering marriage, don't look deep into his gorgeous eyes and say you can't imagine your life with him. Look deep into your problems with him and ask, "Am I ready to make all his problems my permanent problems?"

Chapter 11

16 Ways to Know If You're Dating a Player

Out of all the sixteen ways listed to let you know if you're dating a player, not one will be more convincing than your own gut! Because if you think you're being played, your hunch is probably right. It would take someone with their eyes completely shut, not to be able to spot a player. Players are like neon signs, they draw attention to themselves. They want to be seen.

Remember the saying, everybody plays a fool? That's what the player banks on, you being a fool, so he can play you. And it's best, not to try and turn the tables once you know his game, because becoming a member of the Player's Club just for payback could prove a big loss, down a treacherous road. Because whether you play him or he plays you, there will be no winners. Only losers walk away from a player's game.

If I sound like an authority on players, that's because I am. I once walked into a player's den, and became his wife only to be his prey. By the time I was able to walk out, I knew all the rules and every sign. Once you come face to face with a player and get involved in his game, you'll always be able to spot one.

What Is a Player?

Many women get a player confused with a pimp and a user. A pimp has women working for him. Women pay him. It doesn't matter where she gets the money, as long as she gives it to him. A user is basically a slut. A player is neither of the above. A player is just an average guy, who you could run into at anytime, at anyplace, who has never made a commitment with anyone. And after I have said that, I would like to pause and say this. For instance, maybe you'll be in a relationship with a guy that sounds like a player, but you figure maybe he isn't, since he has made a commitment. Maybe you two are living together or planning to get married. Think again. Players do not commit! When you think they have made a commitment to you, they still are not making a commitment. They will tell you they are. But in their hearts, they have not committed; therefore, they do not feel guilty when they go out and cheat on you.

We are still describing a player, but as I mentioned before, don't get a player confused with a user. A user can be any guy, but it doesn't mean he's a player. And if you're wondering what's the difference between being used or played? It's a big difference. A user is not going to try to win you over before he uses you. He'll just pick you up one night, share a drink and your bed and never call you again. A player on the other hand, would never do that. Their game is different. Their game is to win you over so they can play you over and over. If they can achieve this, it gives them a satisfaction they crave.

Players are the type who just go from one female to the next, in most cases, just for sex, but could keep hanging around and coming back for more sex and other reasons. He is usually good looking and charming. And let's not forget, one of the smoothest talkers you'll ever meet. What he may lack in the looks department, the talk makes up for and vice versa. He usually dresses well and drives a sporty car, and flashes money if he's a working player. And if he's not a working player, since most players don't hold steady jobs, he probably won't be flashing dough, but he'll still be in style, even if he has to borrow his brother's clothes. And above all, he's stuck on himself. He could look like Mighty Joe Young in the face, but you would never convince him of that, because he thinks he's it. And of course, many females have made him think he's it; therefore, in his mind, he is it. If he's ever rejected, he will go all out to win you, only to prove he can; but once you fall completely into his web, he will cut you loose.

Last, but not least, his mind is always focused on his game, and his game is centered around women: lots of women. Yet, his mind is focused on his game, he's nobody's fool, and always has his eyes open to see if he's being fooled. If you fool him, it won't be for long. He can easily spot someone else's game.

The Woman He Will Stick With
Since he doesn't want or has never had to deal with real responsibility, the woman he will stick around with for more than one night will have to be someone with her own house or apartment. Someone with an income. Someone who can be a mother image and take care of him and baby him, because so many of them have never grown up.

Stand Your Ground
To make sure you don't get hooked up with a member of the Player's Club, to get caught up in a player's game, stand your ground by laying down the law at the beginning of any relationship. Yes, the law. The law according to your rules. Clearly state your do's and your don'ts, your needs and wants, and what you will and won't tolerate. By standing your ground, you'll keep a protective shield around you that a player cannot penetrate, he'll never be able to get under your skin. Once under your skin, he sticks like glue.

16 Ways to Know If You're Dating a Player

1. When you first start dating a player, his goal is to hook you right off the bat. He quickly pulls you into his web with his irresistible charm. Being around a charming man is a godsend for most females, and the player knows this. And they pour on all their charm, which will fascinate you as he sweeps you off your feet with sweet compliments, one after another. Kind words from the

way you laugh and say his name, right down to the way you hold your ink pen. He will make you feel like the most beautiful, adored woman that was ever born.

2. He will start out pretending to be Mr. Right by acting and talking like a true gentleman. He will seem too good to be true. You're thinking to yourself "how did I get so lucky!" This man is perfect! If that thought ever crosses your mind, always try to read between the lines, before you crown him "King of Your Heart". If there's no invisible writing, you have found Mr. Wonderful. But if his words are double-talk, chances are, you have come face to face with a player.

3. In the beginning of the relationship, he will always be around. You'll never know exactly when to expect him, because he doesn't always phone first, he usually just shows up anytime day or night. But you'll see so much of him until you couldn't imagine a time that he wouldn't be around. He'll constantly ring your phone, calling you just because. But once he wraps you around his little finger, he will call you because: Because he needs this or because he wants that.

4. All through your relationship, until you kick him to the curb, his lovemaking will intrigue you. Players are usually great lovers, because they have had a number of women in their lives and they usually take the time to listen to exactly what turns their partner on. Bear in mind that if he can make your wildest dreams come true in the bedroom—that's one way to keep you under his spell. And of course, he's looking to be rewarded for his great efforts, looking to be showered with your undying love, loyalty and devotion.

5. He doesn't show much interest in your career. As a matter-of-a-fact, he doesn't show any interest in your work. He knows you have a job, and he's happy you do, but could care less about it. He doesn't want to be bored with the in's and out's of what you do for a living. And he could care less about your hobbies, or any other kind of project that interest you. But, on the other hand, though, he's not interested in what you're doing for a living, he feels that

you should be interested in the ideas he's entertaining. Because of course, he's always talking about some project or hair brain scheme that he needs money for. Your money!

6. He's invisible on holidays. You'll discover soon in your relationship that being with a player on holidays is just like being with a married man. He'll never be around to give you a gift or spend time with you. On special days like your birthday, Valentine's Day, Christmas or Thanksgiving he will have a list of excuses about why he can't see you or why he didn't see you. Why he can't see you? Those days are too down to earth. He might have to come down off his high horse and be a regular guy: give you some flowers, give you a card, go shopping with you for a gift, share a family meal and etc. Players don't do that regular guy thing.

7. In the beginning of a relationship, the first couple of dates, when he takes you out on the town, to eat or to the movies, he will pay for everything. But watch closely after that and see if he continues paying for the dates, because a player will only do the honors one or two times, and after that, you will have to pay your own way, and sometimes his. But if you eat at a fast food or family restaurant where the check is under $15.00, he might pay the bill. But most likely he won't leave a tip. Don't be surprised if he says to you, "I'm short…can you pick up the check?" And if you ever pick up the check for him once, he'll never pick it up again.

8. He never gives you a permanent number where you can reach him. He gives you a number, but he's never at that number, or he doesn't answer that number. Most likely the number he has furnished you with is a pager or a cell phone. You never really know how to get in touch with him. You always have to wait until he contacts you. The calls are always on his time or at his convenience.

9. He never takes you around his family, especially his mother. If by chance, you were to call his mother's house, which you won't, since he'll never give you her number. But if by chance you did, his mother wouldn't know who you are. You don't get invited

over to the family picnic or family gathering. He tells you that you are his woman, but nobody in his family knows about you. And most of the buddies that you have met seem to be in the same mind-frame he is, because the guys he deals with or associates with are players too. Or most likely, you may know none of his associates.

10. He will make sure you are kept in the dark about whatever he is into. You don't know that much about what he's doing when he's not around you; and he's secretive about what he does and makes sure you know nothing about any of his business. If he's doing anything shady, you won't know it, until it hits the fan. He only tells you then, because he needs your help.

11. In the early stages of your affair, he's all talk about this and explaining that. He'll take time to spend quiet times together with you. But after being together for a while, and he knows he has you where he wants you, hook, line and sinker, the kid gloves come off. The bottom line after that, is whatever he can get from you, and whenever the two of you are together, no serious communication takes place. He'll hit the sheets with you and afterward, he doesn't hang around to reassure you of his love. He throws on his clothes and hits the door.

12. After spending a few weeks with him, look for major signs of immaturity, such as no respect for the truth. You'll find that his word isn't worth anything. You'll find you can't depend on him when the chips are down. According to Ann Landers in her book, *Wake Up and Smell the Coffee*, "Maturity means dependability, keeping one's word, coming through in a crisis. The immature are masters of the alibi. They are the confused and disorganized. Their lives are mazes of broken promises, former friends, unfinished business and good intentions that somehow never materialize."

13. After being together for a while, gradually his true self will appear. He won't overwhelm you all at once. He'll pick the right time, right when he knows you're hooked; and he'll unmask himself right before you. And once he unmasks to show his true inconsiderate self, he'll never go back to being that sweet considerate charmer that you fell in love with.

14. He's usually always late coming to see you, if he shows up for the date at all. He could be an hour late, a day late or even a whole week late. He'll finally show up, knowing there won't be too much said. He knows you are not likely to rock the boat because of your fear of losing him.

15. He will start borrowing money from you. The first couple of times, it won't be anything big, and he'll pay you back, setting you up for the kill. He'll borrow big and never pay you back. If you turn him down on that first $10, he won't ask you for $20. Just remember, if he needs to borrow a few dollars, he'll survive without your dollars, let him ask his Mama for the dough. It's wise not to share your financial information with any man, unless there's a ring on your finger and the date has already been set. Otherwise, it's not his business!

16. He's not interested in listening to you talk about your problems; while you're talking, it's like his mind is centered on something else as if he isn't paying you any attention. And his comments make light of your concerns or problems, as if they are no big deal. But on the other hand, he wants you to listen to his problems, because his are more important, of course.

You Can't Change Him

You may feel that your great love for him will change him, so you try to stick it out, even though you are aware of his playing, but usually, nothing can save a player from himself. He's not looking to be saved. He's very content and happy with the way he is. It's his basic make up. Plus he usually has too many women to focus on just one; so it doesn't matter how pretty or how nice you are, or even how wealthy you may be. The bottom line is the same: a player is not going to commit to you, and he usually will never marry. Some players do marry, but same bottom line, he still doesn't commit!

What You Can Do

The best thing you can do if you find you're dating a player, is to break off the relationship as soon as possible, bearing in mind, that a player preys on the power you give to him. So the easier way to send him walking is to take back the power you handed him. According to Dr. Tessa Albert Warschaw, author of *Winning by Negotiation*, "Sometimes we behave as though we expect others to remind us that we have power, to support us when we relinquish it, to award us by not taking advantage of our vulnerability. It doesn't work that way. You have to take care of yourself. It's your responsibility to hold on to your power. Every time you hesitate or needlessly apologize or disparage your own statements, you weaken your power. You give power away whenever you let yourself be intimidated."

It's that simple. Take back your power. Players are takers, and when you stop giving, they are out the door!

Chapter 12

5 Men Tell What Keeps Them in Love

There's nothing more beautiful than being in love and sharing love with that one special person who loves you back. If there's love in your life, it can make up for a great many things you lack. If you don't have it, no matter what else there is, it won't seem like enough.

But sometimes when that once-in-a-lifetime connection clicks and you find yourself head-over-heels in love with the man of your dreams, many times certain love destroyers, those nasty little things like boredom and dishonesty, just to name a few, sneak into your relationship and rip your affair to shreds. You may feel things are moving along just fine, but one day you look around and find yourself staring good-bye in the face. Your sweetheart has fallen out of love with you. But since love is so unique, it doesn't just die. Something has to destroy it! Something like those nasty little love destroyers of course!

What follows are statements from five men telling what keeps them in love. They may contain hints as to what keeps love alive. Take from them what you think you can use and leave what won't work for you alone.

Kevin, 29, Musician/Bartender
"What keeps me in love with my girlfriend of the past six months is how she doesn't judge me or make wisecracks about my lifestyle. We

love each other, but we're coming from totally different angles. She's forty-two, a little older than me—a lawyer—Miss Professional. She wears professional attire and attends business meetings. I don't have a degree in anything. At best I'm dressed in cutout jeans and a tee, and my hair hasn't seen a pair of scissors in ten years. I pay my bills bartending while trying to get my music off the ground. But frankly, I haven't made one dime from my music yet. Because of our relationship, she doesn't have the best relationship with her parents. They think I'm a loser. They think she should dump me for one of those big-time executives she works with. But I'm not worried about that happening. She loves me and accepts me for who I am. To me, that's the greatest love anyone can give you."

Casey, 22, Pre-Med Student
"My girlfriend keeps me in love with the way she gets such a thrill out of the way she thrills me. She's very aggressive and is always in the mood. It's like we're in the same place sexually and I'm never left unfulfilled. Sometimes my studies get sidetracked from thinking about how I can't wait to be with her. Every time we're together, before either one of us undresses, she pleasingly exhausts me orally. It's not just the physical thrill that I enjoy, but it's the knowing—the knowing that my woman wants to do everything she can to please me. It's that special fact that makes me love her more and more."

According to Alexandra Penney, author of *How to Make Love to a Man*, "Making love is really a matter of understanding what your husband or lover wants in a total way. This totality includes his physical, emotional, and mental needs. Rich, full, satisfying lovemaking is one of the basics for the kind of intimate, long-lasting relationship that most of us are looking for or have and want to sustain."

Jessie, 31, construction worker
"She keeps me in love with this huge ego she has given me. Yes! My wife has given me the biggest ego ever. And as you can see, (he rakes his hand through his hair) I think I look okay now. But back when I first met my wife, I had never thought of myself as a hunk and for

some reason would never approach really good-looking women. She approached me; and she's damn good-looking. She was my sister's best friend from college who came to spend the weekend with her one summer. She went out with me and I thought she was doing it as a favor to my sister. We wound up sleeping together that same night and she went wild on me, screaming and crying and calling out my name! I thought she was faking it to stroke my ego. But she wasn't faking it. We have been married for three years and she still has a sensational fit every time we make love. She carries on as if I'm driving her absolutely wild!"

According to Dr. Michael Castleman, author of *Sexual Solutions*, "Silence might be golden in some situations, but lovemaking is not one of them. Deep breathing is a powerful tool for releasing tensions, and the addition of sound to exhalation introduces another dimension that helps many men last longer."

Walter, 24, Model
"I have never been in a serious relationship before, but I must admit this woman has me—for now, at least. For starters, unlike other relationships I have had in the past, I'm never bored with this woman. We seem to have the same huge sexual appetite. But what really drives me wild is all those different designer silk panties. She has at least thirty pairs, different colors with different days of the week on them. Each pair represents something different or extra from our regular lovemaking. For instance, Wednesday's color is emerald green; and I look forward to Wednesdays because she is usually dancing around the candle-lit bedroom playing hide-and-go-seek to soft music with that pair in her hand!"

The insidious thing is that most people assume that sexual boredom is a sign of something else, something more than just boredom. Couples, when they run into sexual boredom, tend to feel that their relationship is breaking up, that their partner has found someone else, or that they themselves are inadequate. All of the above are possible, but unlikely. It's more likely that they are in a rut, a repetitive habit that has taken place so often that they always know what is going to happen next. Life or sex without surprise is boring, but not incurable.

Shannon, 44, Hotel/Restaurant Manager
"What has kept me in love with my live-in girlfriend for the past two years is our close friendship. She is my best friend. We have a unique relationship that is so precious I can't even put into words. All I know is that today if we broke up, she would always be the one I would run to if I needed a shoulder to cry on.

Chapter 13

Don't Give Too Much Too Soon

Will he call tomorrow? That's the question Patricia, a 36-year-old hair stylist of Chicago asked herself when she threw caution out of the window and gave in to Duane, a 34-year-old chef from Chicago, on their first date.

"He was so cute and everything I had ever dreamed of in a man, the way he dressed, wore his hair, his talk, his smile, just everything. When he kissed me on my front steps after our date, I just didn't want him to stop. I invited him inside and we continue our necking in the bedroom. Being with him that one evening was magical, and making love with him was the best sex I have ever had. After he left my apartment that evening, I couldn't wait to hear or see him again. Duane never called back."

Chances are, no matter how level-headed, savvy or pretty you are, you or someone you know have found yourself tangled up in a situation similar to Patricia's, where you met Prince Charming on Friday and danced beneath his sheets on Saturday. You got so wrapped up and swept away with his charm that you threw caution to the wind and took a gamble. Afterward you felt empty, because you have been stripped of center stage. The spot light now shines on him. He holds all the cards. You're left wondering with the million-dollar question that you'll constantly carry around, hanging in the back of your mind: "Will he call tomorrow?"

And even though, he may continue the affair, but if he's ten minutes late calling or ten minutes late arriving for your date, your first thought will be—if he'll call or come at all.

Physical love can be as strong as steel, but it's the glue that seals the bond after the foundation has been laid in place. In the beginning of a relationship, it's the mental love that is the strongest. When a person has a love affair with your mind, they will always come back. Only you possess your mind, but on the other hand, sex can be found anywhere.

In some instances, of rushing in, bearing all, the heart leaps into love before you know if you really even like the person. You have taken a chance and walked out on a limb that could break at any time. And depending on the guy, he may not call tomorrow. Then again, there are many who will; but regardless to whether you went out on your first date or tenth date, you'll always wonder where you stand.

You can't shake these thoughts because you have set yourself up for a fall. Your giving might make him happy, because some men want to have their cake and eat it too; but sometimes when they can have their cake and eat it too, the excitement dies. And after just one slice they'll dump the whole cake.

Let Him Court You:

If he's worth shouting to the world about, he's worth taking it slow, getting it right. Why risk losing the days of wine and roses? Courtship is the time when you can account for, ignore, celebrate, and reconcile individual differences. It is the time to establish trust and intimacy as you begin to learn about each other intellectually, emotionally, and physically.

If you skip courtship, you risk running into anxiety and disappointment. But more to the point, why should you skip it when it's such a wonderful chance to be romantic and playful?

Don't Give Too Much Too Soon:

Don't fall into the trap of jumping right into a new relationship, giving your new prince all your time and efforts, allowing everything and everyone else to be pushed aside, allowing him to be the center of your attention, introducing him to your parents, and all your friends and even your kids after just two or three dates.

According to Dr. Carolyn N. Bushong, in her book, *The Seven Dumbest Relationship Mistakes Smart People Make*, "You send the message that you are not worthy of or equal to him, that his lack of involvement and his lack of reciprocation are acceptable, and that you will tolerate his neglect indefinitely." Stick to your bones, don't drop your plans or rearrange your schedule whenever he calls, leaving your friends and family behind, putting much more time and effort into the relationship than your new love.

Maybe at the start of your affair, you felt something very strong and very special and unique for this new man. Maybe you felt he was your knight-in-shining armor. The Prince you had been waiting for, so it didn't really matter to you that you were jumping in with both feet, taking a chance and giving and investing more in the relationship than him. Forcing intimacy like this distracts us from the work on building a real bond because it lulls us into thinking we have already achieved it.

Develop True Intimacy:

Don't fall into the trap of giving too much too soon and taking a chance of sabotaging your affair before it gets off the ground. Develop true intimacy with him before the physical take over. True intimacy provides a shelter in which we can be vulnerable and open, feel safe, and truly be ourselves. True intimacy develops over time, and although the timing varies from couple to couple, true love never happens overnight.

Don't Force Intimacy:

When you force intimacy—you give the man you're pursuing a very uncomfortable feeling, which could send him walking. Forced intimacy feels unnatural and uncomfortable to the man you're pursuing. And because of this unnatural, uncomfortable feeling, at some point, most likely he'll withdraw from you, and when he does, it will only send you the signal that you need to try harder and harder to win his love. And as long as you are chasing after him and trying to win his love, he'll always be in control.

Don't allow yourself to fall into the trap of giving him too much too soon. Regardless to how gorgeous, how rich or how sweet he may be, stand your ground and take your time to develop a special closeness with him before you leap into intimacy and you still haven't placed your relationship on a solid foundation. In the best of circumstances, having sex too soon makes both partners vulnerable. A woman who has sex too soon sets herself up to chase after the man's approval and force intimacy. The man in this situation is likely to be pressured to continue a relationship, or commit himself to a deeper relationship that he may not be prepared for.

Chapter 14

How to Reassure His Return

Sometimes we look forever and never find the right man; and sometimes we do find the right man only to enjoy his company for a short time before he becomes disenchanted and walks away. Many things can send him packing. Only one thing will keep him coming back! That one thing is [uniquely you] and the loving you can give him. One of the most important parts of falling in love is getting the man to want to see you over and over again. You don't want to throw yourself at him, but neither do you want to leave it entirely up to him to remember you, think of something to do together, and then call you. Some men are just plain busy. Many others have trouble thinking of something to do on a date and won't call until they do.

There are lots of ways a woman can take the initiative. Some are better than others: There's the sexy phone call routine. You call and say, "I've just gotten a magnum of champagne and I'm dying to open it, but I don't have anyone to share it with." Or, "I've been thinking about how sexy you are all day long." This sort of thing always worked for Lauren Bacall in the movies. it might work for you, but there are drawbacks.

First of all, the sexy phone call is almost unavoidably a (right now) proposition, explains Dr. Cabot. And says there's nothing wrong with being spontaneous (if you really are), but what if he has other plans for that evening? If he does, you'll both wind up feeling awkward. Second, the sexy phone call is not real subtle, and you run the risk of sounding a bit desperate. Or there's the ploy of "accidentally" leaving something so he'll have to see you again soon just to return the treasure. For instance, your address book, or your briefcase, or your only winter coat, or your entire makeup kit. Surely no man would be so cold-hearted as to deny you the return, all the better.

The problem is he often knows exactly what's going on. Or your ploy could backfire. I remember once when I was dating my husband, another woman he had been seeing "accidentally" left her address book at his apartment. He was too busy the next day to return it, so he offered to leave it out under a pot where he always kept his spare front-door key. She was to stop by during the day to pick it up but, as it turned out, she didn't get a chance. As it also turned out, I was to meet him at his apartment for a date that evening and he was running late. So while letting myself in with the hidden key, I found the book. I had plenty of time to check out the other woman's address book and she was embarrassed when her obvious ploy didn't work out.

Other times, women would leave their belongings at his place and I would wind up using them. Do you want some other women using your "accidentally" left hairbrush, makeup or perfume? Of course not.

Some women send cute cards, or leave little gifts like special cookies or bread they've baked. While still not subtle, this ploy is less aggressive and a lot smarter. These women are on the right track. A man when rereading your card, or eating the cookies you've baked, will naturally think of you—and favorably.

Some gifts function as gifts only; some do double duty as "memory triggers." An effective memory trigger will make him think of you in the right way—so strongly that he will want to see you again. He will pick up the phone and call you. This the goal.

Subtle Triggers:

A memory trigger doesn't even have to be a gift. Consider a spray of your favorite perfume, sneaked onto his inner pillow or sprayed around his mattress. he smells it and thinks of you. Your special soap in the shower. He washes with it and thinks of you.

The love triggers you will use to remind him of you when you're not around will be directly related to his Love Language: For example, a "coffee-table" book you know he likes. Whenever he sees it, he thinks of you. Equally subtle and effective would be a picture you bought together that hangs on his wall, a special dried flower arrangement, and a video game you play together. Maybe a favorite record with your favorite song or recording artist. A melody you like to harmonize together.

You'll want to leave sensual memories. Something he can touch, or smell, or taste. Home-baked cookies aren't bad, but they're soon gone. Try a bottle of aftershave you've picked out especially for him. Or a new razor that's specially made or well balanced. Take him shopping for a new lounging robe in exactly the fabric he feels most comfortable in. Anything he'll use often and react to sensually when he does.

Chapter 15

7 Secret Ways to Lure Him
With Method Sex

Are you in a relationship with a man who just doesn't seem to be on the same wavelength with you sexually? Sometimes he is, and sometimes he isn't. But one thing for sure, at one time he was more in tune to keeping appointments with the bedroom than he is now. You would like to get him back on track to a more balanced lovemaking schedule.

There's nothing worse than when you are hot and he's not. Sure, you can put on soft music or sexy clothes. You can coddle and beg and coo and seduce. But sometimes it just doesn't work. In spite of your best efforts, he's simply unresponsive. He has a headache, or he's upset.

It's not your fault, but somehow you feel as though you're to blame. You blame yourself because you're not sexy enough, and, or you're too fat or too thin, or you said the wrong thing and turned him off. That simply isn't true. You didn't turn him off. He turned himself off. Maybe he's got his mind on his upcoming performance review at the office, or maybe his mother called and wants him to visit. You really don't need to know for sure, because there is a simple technique you can use to remedy the situation.

What do you say to a man who's not in the mood? How do you get him to feel sexy? The answer is by using a variation. Let's say you've just been out with a terrific man and you feel really turned on but some little voice tells you he's not. You can tell he really likes you, but he's just not feeling sexy at the moment. You sense that he has other things on his mind, which isn't very flattering at this point in the evening. Your self-esteem begins to fade. You wonder if you should just go hide in the back of your closet with a blanket or chalk up one more platonic evening when you feel hot as hell. But there's no need to chalk it off, or to just sit there while he remains polite but distracted. You can get him in the mood with a special technique.

Method Sex

"Method" actors prepare for a performance by remembering life experiences of their own that are similar to those of the character they are playing. By getting in touch with that memory just before performing, they are not just acting, but "reliving" those experiences on stage.

- In the same way the method actor remembers a past sad experience to portray sadness, you can get your man to remember a past sex experience to feel sexy. Try stimulating his memory.

- Ask him to remember a time when he was really turned on. Ask him if he can remember his first sexual experience, or his most exotic.

- Watch the expression on his face. Look for an easing of tension around the mouth and eyes. Perhaps a slight smile. It may take a few questions before he really gets into the subject. Meanwhile, remember the "What and how questions."

- Sometimes a man just won't talk about his past affairs, but you can tell from the expression on his face that he is remembering. He doesn't necessarily have to say a word for "Method Sex" to get him in the mood. (If you're a keen observer, you'll be able to remember your lover's "in lust" expression and file it away for future reference).

- The minute you see signs that he is actually remembering a former sexual experience, touch his hand. By getting him to remember past sexually satisfying times in his life, you will not only be putting him in the mood for sex in the present, you will be creating a useful sexual anchor.

- If he's willing to talk about his experiences, getting him in the mood will become much easier. Of course, if he isn't responding verbally, you will be limited to whatever effect one or two questions might have. Don't press and don't appear to be interrogating him. Unfortunately, his unwillingness to talk about his past sexual activities and love affairs limits your ability to translate the "Method Sex" into a firm sexual anchor.

- Different moods can be created by using different memory anchors. Just as recalling past sex experiences can put him in the mood for loving. By getting him to remember times when he was happily in love, you will put him in the mood to be in love in the present with you.

Some women are afraid to ask a man about his past love affairs, particularly about the sexual experiences. They don't want to know, or find it embarrassing to ask, or want to pretend there were never any other women in his life before.

Getting your man to recall past sexual or love experiences shouldn't be thought of as a threat to your present relationship, no matter how great he says it was. I have known women so insecure that they were threatened even by a man's memory of a deceased lover. But if he's had good experiences with other women, it shows he's capable of having a good experience with you—especially if you're listening and learning. Ask him why it was so good, what was it that he liked the best, and what she did that was really special. You're much better off if you know everything.

Chapter 16

The Plain Truth—8 Secrets to Keep Him Coming Back

Being with that right person and enjoying a loving relationship together is what we all want and hope for. Sometimes we look forever and never find the right man; and sometimes we do find the right man only to enjoy his company for a short time before he becomes disenchanted and walks away. Many things can send him packing. Only one thing will keep him coming back! That one thing is [uniquely you] and the loving you can give him. It's you that makes your evenings of passion special to him. According to noted psychologist, columnist and author Dr. Joyce Brothers, "Sex is not a matter of ejaculation alone for men; at its best, it is a communion. Not every time; but there are those blue moon occasions when sex is so delicious, when love and physical pleasure blend into such ecstasy that he feels apart of you. Those blue moons with a woman he really cares for is what makes sex really special to a man. Although a man can have as strong and satisfying an orgasm with a perfect stranger as he can with the woman he loves, he can never have one of those heart-stirring, blue moon peaks with a woman he does not love. And that is something every woman should know, because it is Mother Natures' way of keeping a man around the house.

The key is to not allow him to become disenchanted in the first place. Men become disenchanted when they feel they are missing something. And when they feel if they are missing something, the grass is always greener on the other side of the fence. They start feeling that they go on the hunt and climb over that fence (break up with you or cheat on you) they will discover all the goodies they feel they deserve. All the goodies they feel are missing from their relationship. Men want to be overwhelmed with sex and everything that allures them to sexiness and romance. They want that sexuality it to be a whole part of their lives. Listed below in their order of importance are the 8 secrets that will keep him coming back for that sexiness and romance.

Sex:

The number one thing that will keep him coming back is sex. Sex is basically on a man's mind ninety-five percent of the time. When it's not on his mind, just the slightest thing can trigger it. Sex thoughts are darting in and out of his head continuously; ask any man you know or associate with the question: "What will keep you coming back?" His answer will probably be something like: "Sex, sex and more sex." Why? It's obvious. God created men to be slaves to sex. The more they think about it, the more they can hunt for it, the more they can get.

Men are usually honest when talking with other guys or a non-associate female about sex. But don't look for your prince charming to be hundred percent open about his feeling and sex. Men want to be proper with the woman in their life, and being boldly honest about how his thoughts are always centered on sex isn't something he thinks will make him look or sound to becoming. So in that case, he'll just say what he thinks he should say or what he thinks you want to Hear him say. We may want to think that the man in our lives wants us for our personality and charm and good looks and etc. And yes, that's all apart of the puzzle. But the bottom line is unchangeable. He wants you for your body. Everything else you have to offer is icing on the cake. If the cake isn't available the icing won't appeal to him.

More Sex:

When it comes to sex in a man's eyes, you're dealing with a double-edged sword. Just like sex is what will keep him coming back, it's also the very thing that will keep him away. You can get hurt if you give in, and you can get hurt if you don't; the key is to know the balance, which is, don't give in too soon. Because even though, it's the one thing he wants and the one thing he craves, if there's no chase, no challenge— he won't think it's worth the time.

The thought of sex, the want of sex and the need of sex are what motivates a man to be a slave to sex. More of a slave to sex than any animal. Anthropologists and other scientists have recently come to believe that it is our sexiness as much as our intelligence that sets us apart and distinguishes us from the rest of the animal kingdom.

Human beings are the most erotic of all mammals. With most animals sex is restricted to the periods when the female is in heat; over a lifetime, those periods do not add up to all that much. But men and women, however, can be sexually engaged with each other fifty-two weeks of the year. It is as if way back in prehistory Mother Nature had searched for the most effective way of protecting mothers and children. Without someone to provide food for and defend the mother and child, they were at the mercy of the wild beasts and predatory males. The mother would have to abandon her infant when she searched for food. This interesting species might not have survived. The obvious source of protection was the male. But how to keep him around? Mother Nature's solution was sex. The day-in, day-out sexual availability of the sensuous female.

Promise of Sex:

Some of us get in a rut thinking our relationship will work out just fine without putting out, and it can work just fine without sex, depending on the situation. But overall, whether you're married or just dating, sex has to be in the mix, or on the list to be thrown in the mix at a future time. If you plan to keep the man in your life coming back, there has to be some kind of understanding that sex will eventually, somewhere down the line, be a great part of your relationship. A man likes the chase when he knows there is a possibility to catch what he's after.

Men may be slaves to their sex thoughts and urges, which is at the very center of their makeup, but the decent thing about a man, if he cares enough for you, is that he will wait for your loving. For you if you are a virgin or just not ready. If you're not ready tell him and let him know where he stands. Don't keep putting him off without letting him know why (you're not ready). It's a female choice to wait, but it's also her responsibility to let the man in her life know why she has decided to wait, so he can decide if he wants to wait along with you.

Sex the Agenda:

Once you have crossed over into the world of making love with him, there's no going back to "I'm not ready." He won't see the need to wait. Once you start and you stop—he's history. Taking sex off the agenda is the one thing that destroys a lot of marriages. Some married couples make mistakes by not keeping [sex] on the agenda, thinking they can maintain a happy marriage without it, letting work, the kids, everything under the sun come first, until they look around and find that they are no longer connected. Sex is the holding glue, and eventually if sex walks out of the relationship, the man will follow.

Being Honest:

To keep him coming back, honesty will have to be apart of your relationship almost as much as sex. Unless a relationship is based on honesty and trust, it can only go in an endless circle, from one conflict to another. Honesty is having integrity and consistency in all that we think, say, and do. Honesty is something that every couple needs in their relationship. Being honest and on the level from the start, there should be no major surprises. Some surprises can lead to mistrust and mistrust can lead to the downfall of your relationship. In any relationship, there will be some surprises. All through your relationship you discover little things about each other. But there shouldn't be a major surprise lurking that will uproot the foundation of your relationship.

Men and women both want honesty in their relationships, but men demand it in a deeper sense. They can't deal with or handle a lie or deal with deceit as well as a female can deal with those things from them. An example, if he lies or cheats on us, just maybe we'll be forgiving. Will he forgive the same betrayal? Not likely!

Lovable Attitude:

Being lovable and good company is right up there at the top of his list of things that will keep him coming back. A friend told me once that he took a lover because his wife was always fussing at him about something. Little petty things. He said his lover was an escape from the negativism he got at home. He didn't take the lover with intentions of leaving his wife; but the sweet attitude along with sex around the clock caused him to divorce her.

Your Sexiness:

Look and dress the part. Be sexy in what you wear, how you wear it and when you wear it. It's not just about styling your hair and dressing to please him, it's about knowing what attracts him and pleases him and trying to be accommodating. If you know he always look twice at women in short skirts and dresses, go out and buy a short skirt and a short dress and strut them for him. Even if you don't like short skirts and dresses, what could it hurt to wear one every once in a while just to see that smile on his face.

Self-Assured:

Your self-assurance will bring confidence and respect for you in his eyes, along with instant sex appeal. Building confidence and respect builds more intimacy; and more intimacy brings more love. Show him how comfortable and self-assured you are with your body. Don't rush to turn off the lights or grab the covers. Let him see, that even though you may not have a perfect figure—you are proud of what you have.

Don't Take For Granted:

No matter how much couples try to keep their relationship in harmony, it will not work, if they can't care and respect each other's feelings. It's vital not to take for granted the nice things he does. Don't fall into a rut of thinking he is supposed to do them just because you're together. Because whether he's supposed to do them or not, if a person continues to do nice things for someone and that person doesn't seem to appreciate or show that they care about what that person is doing for them, the Giver will stop giving, figuring why should they, when their mate doesn't seem to care or appreciate it. Keep your man coming back by not taking him for granted; and by showing and telling him how much you appreciate all the things he does for you.

Chapter 17

Enhance Your Sex Appeal

What is sex appeal? It's attractiveness. Anything about you that appeals to the opposite sex; the something about you that makes him take that second look. Sex appeal is something every female has. Some of us may not know we have it, but it's there whether you realize it or not. The key is to enhance what you have and make it even more appealing than it is. To enhance your sex appeal and feel and look sexually attractive is just a matter of thinking that way. It's a must to think of sexual attractiveness as a way of life. It should be a full-time state of mind and not just an attitude you put on in bed, then toss back into the closet during your everyday life.

6 Tips to Enhance Your Sex Appeal

Play It Up:
We all have a feature about ourselves that we like better than the next and Dr. Bushong explains that we should determine our most special or unique feature, and play it up. "If you got it, flaunt it," says Elaine Fields, Chicago, Illinois, a 37-year-old plus size nurse with a large bust. "I love to wear outfits that compliment my bust size. My breasts are one of my best features and I'm not ashamed to say that I flaunt them to the max." She points to her petite friend who's sitting beside her smiling. "What are you smiling for Miss Pancake Chest? You have a great rear and flaunt it in those tight Levi's like crazy" She pauses.

"Seriously, I don't see anything wrong with trying to look and be your best. A slender associate of mind that I used to hang out with after work told me I was showing too much skin. But she only said that because everywhere we went I was getting more attention than her." She pauses. "So the person who has a problem with that, has the problem. They need to flaunt what they have and maybe then they wouldn't mind seeing the next person flaunt their thing."

Confidence In Yourself:
Having confidence in yourself will enhance your sex appeal, says Michelle Woods, 31, of Detroit, Michigan, clerical worker, "I used to let myself go when I didn't have enough confidence in myself. I would go to work upset and when I got home I would also be upset. I didn't care about myself or anything it seemed except getting recognition from my boss for the hard work I was doing, since the recognition wasn't coming, my confidence in myself dropped and so did my sex appeal. I was too upset it seemed to care about keeping my hair together and keeping myself looking my best. All I wanted was that pat on the back. Then one day it dawned on me that it didn't matter whether I received appreciation from my boss or not. All that mattered was that I knew I was doing a good job. I had to build confidence in myself. After I got out of that rut of looking for a nod from my boss and found more confidence, I started feeling more sexually appealing, because I started taking better of myself."

Just like Michelle was saying, who wouldn't like a pat on the back? You do a good job or a good deed and you want to be recognized or shown appreciation for it. But don't mope if your boss, your mother or boyfriend doesn't show it to you. Give yourself a pat on the back. Who knows better than you how hard you work. Have and show confidence in yourself. Talk and act with confidence and according to Dr. Bushong we should even practice walking with confidence and pride: shoulders back, chest out, eyes straight ahead. Look as if you know where you're going and how to get there. If you don't feel it, fake it until you do.

Cheerful Attitude:

Enhance your sex appeal by putting on a happy face and not allowing little problems to get under your skin and tear you down. Don't be negative. Put a positive spin on life. Nobody likes a person that is always sad and complaining all the time. "I have always been a big boned, larger lady," says Elaine. "And when I was in my twenties I used to feel depressed a lot. I would feel sorry for myself because I couldn't seem to get down to that size seven that I wanted to be. It took awhile but when I finally realized that I was never going to be a size seven, I started feeling better about myself. It wasn't doing me any good to mope around with a depressed attitude. I picked myself up out of that rut and started being more cheerful and appreciating what I have. When I stopped complaining and being a wet sock to be around, my friends started hanging around me more and calling me up, asking me to do things with them."

Look Your Best:

Don't let having a cold, an outbreak of blemishes, or a few extra pounds diminish your confidence. We all know that in order to look or feel sexy we must take pride in taking care of ourselves. Whether your style is a natural, well-groomed look or something more elaborate and sophisticated, always look your best. It tells others, "I care about me and I take care of myself."

"When ever I walk out of my front door, you can bet I'm together from head to toe," says Elaine. "I try to look my best whether I'm going to work, church or just a walk in the park. As a single female I don't know where I might bump into Mr. Right. And I don't plan to bump into him with rollers in my hair."

Always be Yourself:

Don't alter yourself to please others. You will feel more sexually appealing when you are being yourself. For instance, if you buy a dress just because your best friends wants you to, but you really hate the dress, you're not being yourself and pleasing yourself, you're pleasing someone else, you'll be boosting that person's confidence and stepping on your own. You can't be sexually appealing if you're not being yourself. When you're talking to your mate, be as real, honest and direct as you would be with your same-sex friends.

"I feel more sexually appealing when I'm being myself," says Michelle. "When I was younger, I used to alter myself and allow others to pull my string in every direction except the direction I wanted to be pulled. But no more. I'm in charge of my life—being myself and I have never felt more sexually appealing."

Embrace Humor:
We are not all blessed with a sense of humor, but we can all laugh. When we are around friends and family members who tell jokes, we can have an open mind and try to laugh. Cultivate a good sense of humor. Learn to loosen up and laugh at yourself and at life. Humor is a turn-on because it keeps life's problems in perspective.

Chapter 18

12 Secrets to Sizzling Passion

Slowly, like a building tidal wave, the figures on divorce keep mounting. In the course of the eighties, we were first dismayed and then alarmed to learn that fully half of all marriages in the United States would end in divorce,. The dramatic and troubling truth is that this figure is unquestionably here to stay.

But even with the huge rates of divorce, people are still walking down the aisle everyday. They are not less interested in marriage. It is still the most celebrated ceremony in this country. But many couples will walk away from a fading relationship without hesitation once the passion dies, because we want a lifetime of love; we want lasting passion with one special person and when the latter plays out, both men and women would rather risk the pain of divorce than the loss of feelings.

The radiance and the splendor of sweet passion will soothe your relationship and keep your love everlasting just as long as you keep the fire ablaze. The very instance you ignore the fire by thinking it can burn on its own, is the very instance, you blow your passion to the wind, to survive on its own. It may ride the clouds for a while but your affair will be as fragile as a bubble floating in the air. And just like that, the radiance of it all, and the sizzling light that filled your life has faded to black.

Respect Differences:

In our journey toward lasting love and sizzling passion, we must remember to nurture and respect the differences between us. By doing so, it can cut down on many little arguments and spats. Although each of these differences creates a possible conflict; they also create the opportunity to grow together as well. In relationships, we are generally attracted to a person with certain qualities that, in a sense, are either dormant within or yet to come out of us. When we are one way and our partner is another way, we are instinctively attracted to them to help us find balance with ourselves. Finding this balance creates passion and attraction.

Communication:

Communicate your feelings openly and honestly with each other at the breakfast table as well as in the bedroom. Good communication provides a healthily basis for a loving, meaningful relationship. When you share your feelings and thoughts with your mate, you build a bridge, a bond, between you. While you're having sex, compliment your partner with words, sounds, or gestures.

Lots of Appreciation:

Give him lots of appreciation for all the wonderful things he does for you. And don't fall into the trap of assuming he knows how you feel, because your appreciation of him is an essential ingredient that will help him grow in the relationship as well as help to keep your union strong. When your partner does not feel appreciated in the relationship, he also stops growing. He may not know why, but when he returns home he feels increasingly passive and disengaged from his partner.

Clear Sexual Signal:

To keep the passion alive in her man, a woman needs to give him clear signals about when she's in the mood and when she's not. Every man who has passionately loved a woman knows how painful it is to love her and want to make love to her and then feel rejected sexually. If he continues to initiate sex and his partner is repeatedly not in the mood, he then automatically stops feeling his desire for sex with her.

Laughter in the Bedroom:

Sex isn't always skyrockets at night and the earth moving. You simply can't always be transported to new levels of experience. There is a lot in sex that is silly or unexpected or awkward. Laughter gives you safe and happy passage through the less than perfect moments that make up most of our sexual encounters.

Kisses on Tap:

Kissing can be very intimate, because kisses are of course, non-verbal compliments to the person you're kissing, and non-verbal compliments from the party who's kissing you. Talk between kisses. Don't always keep your eyes closed while you're kissing. Keeping your eyes open encourages talking and communicating with sounds, hugs, tugs, murmurs, and moans.

Share Gift of Love:

Whether you have just gone out on your third or twenty-third date, and whether you have decided to wait until after graduation, or after marriage, or just whenever you feel the time is right, sharing yourself sexually with your partner will be your ultimate gift of love. According to Dr. Bushong, "In a romantic relationship, sex is the crucial ingredient that distinguishes the two people who love each other like family from the two who are in love. Because good sex requires the ultimate in vulnerability, trust, honest expression, and total emotional commitment, there is nothing in the context of a relationship that can replace it."

Talk in the Bedroom:

It's not always that easy to tell your partner that they aren't touching you in exactly the right spot, or that you are not that comfortable with being touched in a certain way. It's extremely necessary to try and find a way to communicate your feelings and thoughts in the bedroom, because as uncomfortable as you may feel about it, it's essential to maintaining a satisfying, loving relationship. Pillow talk in a romantic non-demanding way is vital to keeping the sparks flying high at full speed in your affair; otherwise, your silence will keep them doing what they're doing thinking all is well, since there hasn't been any complaints from you. If sex isn't perfect from the beginning, if certain problems exist or if the sex is not as satisfying as they would like, some lovers jump to the conclusion that maybe it's because they're not really in love, instead of seeing it as a possible communication problem.

Keep Lovemaking Fun:

One major step in keeping the passion sparks flying at full sizzling speed in your relationship is making sure you give him lots of loving, as much as his heart desires. But bear in mind, it's not always how often you make love, it's also how wonderful you make each other feel when you do. With that in mind, try and make your romantic times together as much fun as possible. Be playful and carefree and totally giving of yourself, with your mind focused totally into the moment [knowing you are totally focused into your partner—will make that person even more excited] as if the two of you are the only two people alive. The point is to make sex joyful instead of a duty, to make sex loving instead of performing, an occasion for making love instead of just having sex.

Dash of Spice:

Set the scene with sweet smelling candles and soft music in the background, maybe try some satin sheets on the bed, whatever it takes to spice up your routine. Boredom spells the end of good sex—and often of the relationship. One survey, over fifty percent of men and women thinks marital sex is boring; and more than sixty percent of them have at least one extramarital affair. "So to mix a couple of old sayings, an ounce of prevention is better than locking the barn door after the horse is gone."

Variety in Lovemaking:

Variety in your lovemaking will bring spice and excitement to your bedroom, and it's one way to make sure "boredom" doesn't show its dreadful head. According to author Alexandra Penney, in her book, *How to Make Love to a Man*, that dreadful head of "Boredom is one of the biggest problems men have with their love interest. The woman who puts on her face cream and wears the same gown night after night and does the same routine in the same room at the same time is asking for trouble. Use a little a imagination and give him some variety." And a little imagine can go a long ways, like different positions and different times. Don't set patterns, use candles, different rooms in the house, and different pieces of furniture. By becoming more sexually exciting yourself, and by opening yourself to new sexual activities, you may find a sexy person you really like—yourself.

Sample Gourmet Lovemaking:

This special treat is for those very special evenings when you both are very rested, like during days off work or vacation. And as long as you both are comfortable with it, this could be those special occasions to share each other's fantasies, and try and make each other's fantasies come true. Gourmet sex requires not only deliberate preparation, but oftentimes-special accessories. Finally, even the best of gourmet cooks would not want to go to the trouble of preparing an elaborate meal every night. It would simply require too much energy and time. It would soon become tedious and might even be experienced as a burden rather than a treat.

Integrate some of the twelve secrets into your relationship and watch the sparks in your affair fly. Passion is the spice of a loving relationship, and when it fades out, so does the relationship!

Chapter 19

12 Secret Ways to Become a Romantic at Heart

Some people are romantic, and it comes as easy and as natural to them as breathing. Some people are not romantic and would like to be, but don't know if they can be. But anyone can be romantic and become a romantic at heart, and all it takes—is learning how to be romantic in actions and in thinking. According to America's romance Coach, Gregory J.P. Godek in his book, *1001 Ways To Be Romantic*, "Romantics have a good sense of humor. There's no such thing as a humorless romantic." While the foundation of romance is a serious love, the nature of romance is lighthearted. Romantics are passionate. I'm not talking about sexual passion here, but about a passion for life. Romantics don't allow their lives, or love lives, to slide into boredom—the deadly enemy of all relationships. Romantic are more sexually passionate than the average person. Just another of the many side-benefits of the romantic lifestyle!

The key to becoming a romantic at heart is to do as the romantics do. Romantics "work at it"—and "play at it," too! Being a romantic is not the same as being a starry-eyed, unrealistic dreamer. Romantics often work long and hard to pull off some of their "romantic masterpieces." Romantics plan and scheme, buy gifts ahead-of-time, search for sales, and stock-up on greeting cards. Romantics are always dating.

Daily Romantic Checklist:

Thoughtful Calls:
One of the first things toward becoming a romantic at heart is to start picking up the phone and calling your sweetheart more. Romantics are always using the phone lines, keeping the airwaves busy with sweet nothings to each other. Shirley Woods, 48, Nurse, of Dearborn, Michigan agrees. "When my boyfriend and I first started going out, he would give me a call everyday at work. We wouldn't cat line, but he would call just to say hi and ask how my day was going. Getting those calls from him would make me feel more romantic. When he stopped calling, I thought something was wrong with our relationship. He said he stopped calling because he didn't want to bother me at work, plus I never gave him any calls at work. When I explained how I looked forward to those calls and how they made me feel more romantic—he started back to calling me and I started calling him some time as well."

Make a point of putting yourself in the habit of checking-in with your special fellow—at least once during the day. You're just calling to say "Hello" or to see how his day is going. We all love to be thought of, and men are no different when it comes to receiving a thoughtful call.

Say, I Love You:
It's not always easy for some individuals to say these words to the one they love. But saying them is one of the most romantic things you can say to your partner. Put your—self in the habit of saying "I love you" to your man. Just saying those words will make you feel like more of a romantic. The more you say it the better, at least three times at day: During breakfast, dinner and right before bed.

"Not hearing these words was one of the main reasons I divorced my husband. I really didn't want a divorce. I loved him and I wanted to make it work. But for so many years, I had starved to hear those three words from him. He never reassured me with his words and actions that he loved me," says Shirley Woods.

Most of us can never get enough of being reassured that we're loved by the one we love; hearing those three words "I love you." And, girl-friend, it works both ways, your man wants to be reassured as well.

Loving Compliments:
A single compliment can mean so much to the man in your life. We love compliments from the man in our life, compliments make us feel loved and special. Give your partner compliments on a daily basis and make him feel loved and special. All you have to do is say things to him that you would like for him to say to you. Compliment his hair, or clothes when he dresses for work or dresses up for the evening. Compliment his smile when he's sitting across from you at the dinner table. You can also tell him every once in a while how hand-some he looks and how nice he smells.

Private/Quiet Time:
Private/quiet time is not always so easy to squeeze in between work and the kids. But these times together is one way to keep your bond and romance alive. Make an all out effort to spend at least an hour of uninterrupted time with your mate every evening. Accept no excuses! Make it happen! Talk about loving things and not your day-to-day hassles. Discuss those hassles and real problems like bills and the kids any other time. This is the time to tell him how much you appreciate and treasure his love, and having him in your life. Quiet/private time can be spent just snuggling or hugging or kissing.

Say Thank You:
Whenever you do something nice for someone and they say "thank you." It makes you feel that your favor or gesture was appreciated. That's the way your partner will see your "thank you." Saying "thank you" to a man will score a lot of points in keeping him feeling appreci-ated. And when he's feeling appreciated he will feel more romantic, according to Dr. John Gray in his book, *What Your Mother Couldn't Tell You & Your Father Didn't Know*, "While a woman feels romanced by the flowers, chocolates, etc., a man's sense of romance is fueled by a woman's appreciation of him. When he does little things for her and

she appreciates it a lot, then he feels more romantic." Let him know his love is appreciated. Thank him on a daily basis for the many things he does for you, and keep his sense of romance sizzling.

Unexpected Gifts:
When you are given an unexpected gift, it probably makes you smile. And when you give someone an unexpected gift, it probably always has a way of putting a smile on that person's face. Set a timetable for yourself. On a weekly basis, if possible, to bring home one small, unexpected gift or present for your mate. It doesn't have to be expensive. The idea is to give any simple token just to express your love.

Lovemaking:
Romantic individuals spend a lot of time in the bedroom, besides sleeping. Becoming a romantic at heart, means you need to keep this activity at the top of your priority list. One more thing, keeping appointments with the bedroom isn't quite enough. You also have to make sure you don't allow boredom to sneak into your relationship. You would think, that a couple in love wouldn't need to worry about boredom. But if that was true, we wouldn't have so many couples leaving each other because their passion flame has faded out. The passion flame fades out because routine brings boredom. And boredom kills passion. As often as you can, have a special spot for your lovemaking. A different spot can be anything from a hotel room to a secluded beach. But if you can't leave home, a different room in your house can bring the same excitement: On the sofa, on the kitchen floor, on the living room floor in front of the fireplace.

A Night Out:
Being a romantic at heart means getting out and spending a night on the town, allowing yourself to be wined and dined, enjoying the sights and sounds that a full romantic evening often. Don't allow your relationship to fall into the rut of becoming stale. All too often, after a couple walk down the aisle or has been coupled for a while— they think of going out as a luxury instead of a must. Everything else has a higher priority than their fun-time. Spending nights on the

town get thrown over in their "things to do basket." When you start putting off fun times together, for whatever the reason, it's a strike against your relationship. A strike toward putting a wedge between the two of you. Spending a night out as often as you can will serve as much needed spice in getting and keeping the excitement and romance in your relationship.

Mail Something:
Go shopping for fancy greeting cards, and put yourself in the habit of mailing that special man in your life cards and loving notes. You can do the same even if you're married or living together. Imagine his face when he receives a card or note in the mail from you with a bear and say "This is me. Hug me and care for me."

Upcoming Weekend:
Romantic couples are always doing things and spending time together. Make weekly plans for each upcoming weekend. Always have things planned that the two of you can do. Keeping busy together and doing different things together add adventure to your relationship and keep your romance blooming. Anything from simple plans like visiting museums, parks and zoos to the more expensive, like a cozy resort.

Romantic Surprise:
Plan one romantic surprise each month. Here are two suggestions: Pack a basket with lots of goodies including cheese, crackers and champagne on ice, and take a drive out to the country and have a champagne picnic under a big tree on a sunny hillside. Rent a boat for two or three hours, it's not as expensive as you think. Take a cruise out on the water and enjoy the cool breeze against your face while enjoying each other and a cold glass of wine.

Discover Restaurants:
Eating out or in, is one of the things at the top of a romantic person list. Dining out to dim lights and candle light with soft music in the background, or sitting on the balcony or patio of a cozy café, taking in the fresh air and the sun, enjoying a meal together, is all romantic. A couple enjoying a meal together is one of the most romantic things

two people can do together. But just like anything else, if you keep going back to the same restaurant, often sitting at the same table—it can become to routine and lose its warmth. So, as much as you enjoy your regular restaurant, it can lose its appeal after awhile if you don't add variety to your list. Get into a routine of seeking out different cozy eateries to dine at once or twice a month. Many times there are little cozy restaurants right in your area that you have never checked out. A new and different place for dining can add sparkle to your romance.

Chapter 20

5 Romantic Surprises to Dazzle Your Man

Dazzle your man with romantic surprises and keep your relationship on a smooth, sweet, exciting captivating sail forever. For any relationship that hopes to last the long haul of the day in, and day out existence, variety in the romance department will have to fit into the picture. Variety is that miracle link to survival for any long lasting relationship. Repetition is the dark destroyer that shoots down affairs.

Let down your hair and roll out the red carpet for your relationship. If you're not sure you want to dazzle the man you're with, and do the loving gestures that romantic surprises entail, then maybe you're not sure you want to be with the one you're with. It's not easy to relax in the arms and be totally romantic and playful with someone you're not sure of. Especially if you consider the man in your life a passing fancy, until Mr. Perfect come along. If that's your train of thought, put yourself to this quick quiz: Does he treat you nice? You can't honestly see a valid reason to break up with him? He's the only man you're dating? He calls you on the phone more than any other guy? If you answered yes to every question—he's the one! There's no Prince Charming or Mr. Perfect right around the corner.

If you have been dating someone for a while, and you're considering getting serious, but you're not sure that he's really everything you're looking for. You evaluate your relationship with this simple formula: 70% +spark = A-OK. In other words, if this person has at least 70% of the qualities you want your ideal partner to have, plus you have 'spark' passion and romance; you're soul mates. You click. Go for it! You know you're not going to get 100%! There are no perfect men! "But don't settle for less than 50%," says author Greg Godek.

Now, that's settled. He's the one who is there for you and loving you. Make the most out of your relationship and dazzle him with romantic surprises. Show him how much he means to you.

Risky Affairs:

As much as men love romance and making out, they can be extremely shy when it comes to displaying it in public. In that case, with your man in mind, consider this risky affairs approach similar to playing poker. Never tip your hand before time; keep all your cards close to your vest and slowly, casually surprise him with some risky affairs: meaning, romance and seduction in unusual places like, in the back of a limousine, on the train, at the beach, on a picnic, in the pool, on a boat, in a store dressing room, your bathtub, the fire escape, on the porch, the rooftop, the kitchen floor. Managing to steal a few kisses and touches in all the right spots in such risky places will set your man on fire. When he finally gets you behind closed doors—his passion will fly through the roof. Go on! Dazzle him with risky affairs. But listen closely! Don't get caught!

Sensuous Talk:

On occasions, before, during and after your lovemaking, talk about sensuous things, anything from the way he's making you feel when you're making love, to how sexy he looks when he undresses. What you enjoyed about last night. This skill can keep your sex life lively. By stating aloud what is going on and how it makes you feel, you give your partner pleasure and a sense of security. And this is very arousing.

Sensuous Caressing:

One quiet evening, dazzle him with the idea of a full body massage. The two of you can enjoy each other in this extremely romantic adventure. Giving each other a full body massage is a romantic change of pace to relax and pamper each other. Set aside so much time to indulge and treat each other to pure pleasure. Pleasuring involves exploring the body to test every possible part of sensitivity before rushing into making love. Take turns touching each other all over. Between the touching and caressing, take time to enjoy a glass of sweet red wine or icy cold champagne. After sipping your wine or champagne, try moving your fingers more slowly than usual to increase the intensity of every touch. Caress the feet with your whole hand. Move up the leg, touching ankles, calves, and inner and outer thighs—first with a light touch, then harder. Now concentrate on the lower and upper back and neck. Massage the hairline, head and ear-lobes. Move to the front and lightly touch the stomach with light kisses.

Place An Ad:

Place a personal ad to that special man in your life and list it in your local newspaper under the personal column. Let your man know why he is so special. This will not only surprise him, it will also intrigue him, knowing you cared so much to go through the loving trouble. Write your love message in code, possibly using your private pet name for him. This gives you a great opportunity to dazzle him with a special romantic surprise. You can express your feelings in just a few loving words. When the ad appears, circle it and leave it on the kitchen table when you leave for work. If you're not living together, call him at work on the day the ad appears and tell him there's a secret message for him on a certain page of the morning paper.

Seductive Meals:

Surprise him with a romantic dinner on the floor in front of the fire-place. If you don't have a fireplace, try the balcony at dusk and watch the sunset while you eat. If you don't have a fireplace or balcony, the middle of your living room floor will do. Think of this meal as foreplay. If you don't want to go out, set a table at home or, if you are in a hotel, order room service. Eat by candlelight. And for this seductive, sensuous meal, serve sensuous foods. Foods that are sweet and tasty you can lick right off your fingers and eat out of hand. Finger foods like small fruits: cherries, grapes and strawberries; they have a nice sensual feel to them. Foods you can eat with your hands and serve each other like, finger sandwiches and cut vegetables with exotic dips. And during this romantic meal, you should "take turns describing the things you like about the way your partner makes love to you." It's the perfect time. You're alone in a candlelit room with soft music. Describe what you like about this passion and lovemaking in vivid details.

Chapter 21

Indulge His Senses in True Romance

There's a saying that the French are the world's greatest lovers, taking their lovers to the height of ecstasy. And the reason for the saying, no doubt, is that many of them live by some of the romantic secrets and sizzling legends that were left behind by the great French Courtesans, who were known famously back in the 19th Century.

You, too, can take your man to the height of his desires and entice his mind as well as his body, by learning the secrets of the French, which is basically no more than the basic art of indulging all of a man's senses in true romance.

Why concentrate on his senses? Because all five of a man's senses are essential to his sexual makeup and any one of them can cause him to be totally aroused at the drop of a hat—from the sight of your sexiest outfit, the touch of your soft, clean hair, the smell of your favorite perfume, the sound of your voice saying his name, the taste of a delicious dinner you prepared, or the taste of your smooth lips against his.

Now consider your own senses, how you appreciate the taste of a sweet dessert, the smell of a rose, the touch of his skin beneath your fingers, the sound of his voice when he calls you. Your senses live and breathe romance just the same as his, but there's one major difference! Now imagine his overwhelming excitement when you indulge all five of his senses in true romance—allowing your man to be lost in romance from the moment he steps into your bedroom from the sight of a single candle flickering, to the scent of fresh yellow roses, to the sound of soft romantic music, to the touch of the cool satin sheets against his skin—to the taste of your sweet strawberries and cream and icy champagne on the bedside table.

Sense of Sound:

Catering to his sense of sound can make your man's imagination zoom to the sky. Ever wondered why chat lines are so popular with men? Listening to a sexy voice drives him wild. "Wild is probably the right word," says T.J. Jones, 25-year-old Rapper from Detroit. "We can be in the middle of a big money deal and just one familiar sound can focus our mind right toward the bedroom. Like the sound of a zipper being undone. Even hearing a word you use everyday being used in a sensuous voice. My girlfriend was standing in the bedroom door one evening while I was watching football. I glanced at her standing there looking at me with a can of pop in her hand. She said, 'You want to share this can of pop with me?' Right away, football or no football, I couldn't resist. I had to share that can of pop with her; because from the sound of her voice, I got the real picture; and it wasn't soda pop!"

Enticing his sense of sound can be anything from learning what music he enjoys, and having it playing on the stereo when he comes over, to giving him the sweetest pillow talk, to your soft breathing against his neck, to moans and cries of pleasure when you're wrapped in passionate lovemaking.

Make sure to keep your eyes and ears opened and pay attention to what kind of music seems to get his attention. This way you can choose the type of records and tapes that he will be able to respond to. If he's involved in Pop, Soul, Rap, or Blues, playing Hard Rock most likely wouldn't be an appropriate gesture.

Sense of Sight:

His sense of sight is an obvious razor sharp arousal giant. We've all seen how men keep their eyes glued to females as they walk down the street. Some men can't take their eyes off of a women's breast, some pay close attention to a woman's butt, and some notice a woman's legs or her beautiful hair. And we have all noticed how men love to look at sexy, provocative pictures in certain adult magazines. Men's responses vary widely, but in general most men quickly react to visual stimuli. Keep in mind, however, that what stimulates one man could cause embarrassment to another; size up his particular likes and dislikes or get to know his preferences and please him accordingly.

You to can easily set some warm and enticing scenes for your man at home: Turn your bed down the way it's done at popular hotels, arrange a romantic table setting with candle-light and fresh cut flowers, have a warm, sweet smelling bubble bath waiting for the two of you, when he comes home, place one of your sexy nightgowns across the bed or over your bedroom chair, place a magazine of provocative pictures on the bedside table where he is sure to see it.

Make sure he gets a full view of you wearing your sexy nightie. When it's time to shed it, do it slowly so he can enjoy the sight of you undressing. Don't be shy, keep lights turned on! He wants to see all of you. "That's right. What is she shy for? If I'm with her, it means I want to be where I am. It means I like every inch of her," says T. J.

Sense of Smell:

Many men out there, and maybe including yours, are not as aware as women are of the huge power of perfume and its aphrodisiac effects. Indulge his sense of smell by giving him a bath with some scented bath oil, place a fragrant soap at the sink, spray your sheets and pillows very lightly with the fragrance that you use. Dab some of the perfume you wear the most on the light bulbs; when the bulbs are turned on, the heat will float the scent throughout the room. We all know that fragrance is a very powerful subliminal signal that makes a man aware of your presence, but use it lightly. Just the right amount can be magical.

Sense of Touch:

A man's sense of touch by far ranks at the top of his list as the ultimate sense. This sense is the one he would pick over all the others. To indulge his senses of sight, sound, smell and taste with touch would only keep him around or coming back for so long. The sense of touch has to be in the mix to complete his ultimate fantasy. "If I could only have one of my senses, touch would be the one I would choose," says T. J. "Life wouldn't be worth living if I couldn't enjoy the sensation of holding a woman in my arms."

Any man would tell you that he loves the feel of slippery, silky and satiny material. Those materials are smooth, soft and feminine, and therefore, to a man, very sexy. That explains why so many of them respond to silky, see-through nightgowns and soft sheets that feel smooth and satiny. Men like the feel of fragile glasses and delicate plates and cups also. Those items have a feminine feeling about them that men find seductive to the touch.

"The worst thing a woman can wear to bed with me is a cotton night gown. Some of them look okay and they may be comfortable to her. But this is about a man's sense of touch, right? Cotton nightgowns do absolutely nothing for me," says T. J.

Set a date to go shopping for a few silk and satiny nightgowns if you don't have any, Victoria's Secret has a huge selection. Allow his sense of touch to savor the feel of your silky night-wear, as his hands move over your body to rest on your skin.

Sense of Taste:

We have all heard the saying that, the quickest way to a man's heart is through his stomach. And that saying seems very close to the truth. Since no man seems to deny it. Enjoying a delicious meal would have to be one of his true wonders—only second to making love. So it would be safe to say, preparing a tasty meal for him will rank high on his scorecard.

As far back as time can take us, the sharing of food always seemed to form a connection between people. Think of the first Thanksgiving, something we still celebrate to this day. But even so, we have to keep in mind that just like ours—every man's sense of taste is highly individual. Some men appreciate the time and effort that go into making a candle-lit meal. Others will respond to the thoughtfulness that you prepared their favorite dish, even if it's only a grilled cheese sandwich to be enjoyed with their preferred brand of beer.

The bottom line is that it's his taste you're trying to enhance. Don't slave over a hot stove assuming he'll enjoy what you're preparing. Find out the kind of dishes he enjoys and serve those.

Now that you know his secrets, you to can indulge your man's senses in titillating romance, and watch his heart melt into yours right before your eyes. You'll be able to make your evening together unforgettable, being the first thing he thinks of when he awakes and the last thing on his mind when he falls asleep.

Chapter 22

10 Ways to Indulge Your Relationship in True Romance

To indulge your relationship in true romance, simply means opening up your heart and your mind to receive and give romantic gestures. Romantic gestures are like bees are to honey. They are half of the pie that keeps the passion in your relationship glowing with radiant rays of warmth. These loving gestures come from your heart. You're not doing them for a reward or to be noticed, you're doing them to let your partner know how much you love and appreciate him. They are simply your expressions of love.

To be truly romantic and give your heart completely to another, means taking a risk to wear your heart on your sleeve, which could easily be used as a punching bag or thrown to the ground and crushed. But that's the gamble we have to take, opening up ourselves and revealing our true feelings.

If you are purposely choosing not to open up with your mate—you might want to ask yourself what you're afraid of or what's holding you back. Because, when you think about it, if you're not going to be romantic and open up, then what's the point of being in a relationship with that person.

Indulging your relationship in romance and being more romantic enhances your ESP, says author Godek. Those of us who are tuned-in to our lovers—those of us who listen well—develop a kind of (sixth sense) about what our lovers would love. One of the best things about long-term relationships is that you develop this sense. And as it develops, your relationship deepens and your intimacy grows.

Staying Lovers:

Keep lovemaking at the top of your list, and center it back into your relationship as a main event the way you used to when you first started your relationship. If you and your partner have drifted away from the lover's lane, and you're not currently living as lovers, put forth a great effort to recapture the glow, the passion and the excitement. It's basically a mindset, followed by a few active gestures. Many young couples and others couples starting new relationships, start out as lovers, and many older couples who drifted away from the bedroom have re-discovered that they can still be lovers.

Time in Bed:

On some occasions spend all day in bed doing things other than sleeping and making love. You can read the newspaper together, read the funnies aloud to each other. You can enjoy a light breakfast in bed. Make passionate love and take a catnap together. Snuggle in each others arms and watch old movies on the VCR or TV. Later you can order a Chinese supper; and cuddle up and make love again before retiring.

Cover the Clocks:

Indulge your relationship in timeless romance by covering up all the clocks in your house for the entire weekend. Park your car in the garage, or around the back of the house or the apartment building, or park down the street. Pull all the shades and close all the blinds. No one will disturb you. You can create your own little mini-vacation in the privacy of your own home, that won't cost you the hassle of a trip and spending money, by simply freeing yourself from the trap of the clock. You will be able to indulge yourselves totally into each other, free from the dreaded schedules and appointments.

Gourmet Take-Outs:

When you have invited him over for a romantic meal, but you're short on time and know you won't be able to prepare a delicious, meal yourself, but you don't want to take away from the romance or the moment by serving fast-food or pizza, look for one of those [over-the-counter gourmet] shops. They're becoming quite popular nowadays as our lives can't seem to find enough hours in the day to do what we have to do. The little shops are also known as [guilt-free take-out]. You can get delicious, nutritional meals that are hassle-free, therefore, devoting more time and energy to creating the perfect romantic atmosphere and paying more attention to your mate instead of your oven.

Sweet Surprises:

Men have a special quality of being like little boys at heart, and they never seem to out grow that deep thrill for sweet surprises.

Sweet romantic surprises are an essential part of the romantic way of life. Put effort into making your everyday lives into the captivating, unexpected. Call him at work or school and tell him the next time you get together you'll have a nice surprise for him. Telling him that will peak his interest and keep him looking forward to seeing you. So the point is not to tell him what the surprise is, until he knocks on your door. Maybe on a warm night, you could have a champagne picnic in the backyard under the moonlit sky. If the weather doesn't permit the after-hours picnic, enjoy a warm, soothing bubble bath for two. Make arrangements to plan one surprise for next week, one for next month.

Visit Card/Gift Shops:

Hang out in a variety of stores like, card shops, music stores, lingerie departments, trendy gift shops, magazine stands and bookstores. You don't have to go often—just occasionally. Drop in and hang out every once in a while. Why? To find out what's new! And to spark your creativity. It helps if you put yourself into environments that encourage a romantic attitude.

Get-Away Weekend:

Getting away for a surprise weekend is so romantic, it's considered by many to be a romantic classic. A get-away weekend doesn't mean you have to leave the city or state. You can take advantage of some of your nearby hotels and motels. Many of them have weekend packages. Sometimes these packages are referred to as "Marriage-Saver Weekends" or "Lovers Escape Weekends." If you're not interested in one of the hotels or motels in the area, maybe seek out a romantic bed-and-breakfast inn. Make sure to have both of your bags already packed when he gets in from work, grab him by the hand and lurk him away to your romantic surprise get-a-away weekend.

Writing Love Letters:

You may consider yourself a lousy writer and therefore, you prefer not to write. But whether you write a good love letter or not, isn't the point, the point is to write him a love letter or poem in your own handwriting on one sheet of paper which has been cut in the shape of a heart and glue it to cardboard. After the glue dries, cut it up into small puzzle size pieces and mail all the pieces to him in an envelope. Enclose a note that says, "Here are the pieces to my heart; mend them together and discover how I feel about you."

No Complaining:

One of the sweetest romantic gestures a woman can do for her man is to overlook his shortcomings for a day or maybe even a week. Men love it when women don't nag or complain too much. They may have it coming, but make a mental effort to indulge your relationship with this gesture, and it may just change your life! Decide how much time you're going to close your eyes to his 'mess-ups', whether one day or one week, stick to it and try being totally positive, accepting, supportive and non-judgmental. No complaining or nagging.

Discover New Places:

Most of us live in areas that we have hardly discovered. Buy a guidebook for the community where you live and visit someplace you've never been before. Discover new restaurants, hotels, gift and card shops, bookstores, new music stores and parks.

Indulge your relationship in true romance and become the biggest fan of that special person in your life, because you're providing him with your constant encouragement and unconditional love. You may not succeed at your efforts all of the time, but the point is that you're trying!

Chapter 23

Stay in His Thoughts— Become His Habit

Many things in life can be predicted; and many things in life can be scheduled and many others can be planned; but there's one thing that happens in life, that neither man nor machine can predict, schedule or plan, and that's the all powerful "Love." Love is a mystery to us all and has remained a mystery since the beginning of time. It just happens. You wake up one day and suddenly you love and want to be with another human being more than anything else in the world.

Once we have found that love we would like to stay the apple in his eyes. To remain the apple in his eye, we need to plant a seed here and there. Planting a seed, doesn't mean it's going to grow. But, on the other hand, if we don't plant any seeds, we know for sure that nothing will be growing.

According Dr. Tracy Cabot in her book, *How to Make a Man Fall In Love With You*, understanding the factors that make love a habitual, necessary part of a man's life can help you secure your love relationship. You can become a habit with him, if you know how habits are formed.

One of the main ways both men and women form habits is by repetition. Any act, repeated in the same way over and over again, becomes a habit, a minor addiction. Asking the question have you ever noticed how many habits and minor addictions you have? Coffee, cigarettes, maybe certain kinds of foods and preferred times of day for eating. Your own way of hanging your clothes and organizing your refrigerator. You may be addicted to television news or a morning newspaper. You may be addicted to exercise or hot baths or lying in the sun. Almost all of these habits have been developed over years and years through repetition. Men are particularly susceptible to repetition. They like rituals and the security of knowing everything will be the same.

You may have always thought that men want something new and different and exciting all the time. Not true. When it comes to a lifelong relationship, what they really want is security and happy, predictable regularity. In order to become a habit with a man, you will want to bring a little repetition into your relationship.

That means you should begin to plan your dates for certain nights of the week—every Saturday and Wednesday night, for example. If you miss one night, he'll find his habit interrupted and then he'll be yearning for you.

Through repetition, you can become his habit and addiction. Repetition doesn't come at the beginning of your relationship. it comes at a time when you're nearly ready to make a commitment with someone.

One way to tell if your love affair is ready to progress to something more involved is whether or not there is a regularity to the amount of time you spend together. Men seldom marry the women they see every once in a while. Usually it's the steadily growing love relationships that lead to marriage. Notice how many couples play the same music over and over again. It's "our song" they're playing. They can stand listening to it so many times because it is their personal "love experience trigger." For them, it is highly pleasurable. Through this addictive repetition, the song and the experience both become habitual parts of their lives.

Some couple say the magic words, "I love you," a lot more than others. This verbal repetition gives these couples a better chance of becoming a habit with each other. You could say, "You can see how much I love you." You might say, "You can hear how much I love you." Or say, "You can feel how much I love you."

You have heard the old advice that the way to win a man is to praise him—that men can't get enough flattery. Truthfully, he likes the flattery, but what he really likes is the constant repetition of the loving feeling he gets from being flattered. Flattery doesn't have to be vacuous or fawning. With a little loving thoughtfulness, it can come naturally and steadily, as you get to know each other better. For example, "Hey, that's yummy salad dressing. I like your brand better than mine." Or, "That's a clever way you've arranged your shoes. I never would have thought of that." Or, "What you said yesterday? Well, you were right."

One way your Mr. Right will become addicted to you is through the repetition of all the little pleasant habits and feelings he will associate with you. This will give him a feeling of stability and emotional security he doesn't get anywhere else in the world. Naturally, he'll feel driven to come back to you time and time again. He will become dependent on the regularity of the love he receives. Like a drug addict, he will know there is predictable, repeated pleasure in being with you.

Chapter 24

8 Tips for Driving Him Madly In Love

Meeting that special man who makes our heart sing and being a part of a meaningful relationship is what most of us desire. But meeting and connecting is only half of it, in order for any affair to have any real lasting power, it needs love in the mix. Not just you crazy for him, but his heart pounding for you as well. Love will be the bridge that helps you across troubled times. No matter what type of man it is who attracts you and is attracted by you, the key to whether the attraction will last is love. Love is the "crazy glue" that holds a couple together and strengthens the relationship year after year.

Don't sit around and bite your fingernails wondering if your boyfriend is going to be sticking with you, just make sure he does, by driving him madly in love. According to Dr. Brothers, driving him madly in love isn't as hard as you may think. There's a thin line between love and like where men are concerned. Men are almost heartbreakingly susceptible to love. A man seldom contracts a mild case. He falls head over heels into raging romance. A man usually succumbs to first-stage love long before his love object does. It has been established that men fall in love faster than women. When researchers took the *romance measurements* of 250 young men and 429 young women, they found that more than a quarter of the men had fallen seriously in love before their fourth date, but only 15 percent of the women had.

Be Who He Adores:

Every woman after awhile begin to see what pleases and excites her man—some of the things you may can do, some you may not can do, and some you may not want to do. But give it your best shot to do those things that you feel you can do. Those things that you feel comfortable doing. For example, if you know he always look twice at women in short skirts, and even if you don't like short skirts, strut one for him every once in a while.

Romance Him Blind:

When it comes to romance, some men seem clueless. But they're not. They know what romance is all about, they just think it sounds too girlish. They may quickly say, "That romance magazine isn't for me. I read sports." But when you bring romance to them in term of a candlelight meal or sitting in front of a fireplace enjoying a slow flame, it's right up their alley. He may turn down many things, but romance isn't usually one of them. Put romance at the top of your agenda during your times together, and driving him madly in love will be just your next champagne candle-light dinner away.

Exhaust him with romance in every way possible from putting little love notes in his pocket or briefcase to walking in the moonlight. And if you're wondering why do you need so much romance to get to "I love you?" Because Romance is the process. Love is the goal.

Be Proud of Your Body:

A man is very visual and gets great pleasure from seeing his partner at ease with her body. You may look and feel sexy in your silky nightwear, but what your man thinks is sexy is you getting out of it and feeling comfortable doing so. What they really think is sexy is the woman who is confident and feels good about herself and body. It's all a matter of attitude. Whether you feel attractive has little to do with the size of your breasts or the shape of your thighs. Try to fix your attitude to be proud of your body, and don't insist on turning off the lights or hiding under the covers. Doing so takes away from the moment and you won't be able to lose yourself completely in bed.

111

Keep the Home Fire Burning:

Men want and expect lots of loving from their mate. We all know what can happen if their needs are not being met, not to say that all men will stray if the home fire isn't burning, but why give him any reason to look else where for his warmth. Giving him plenty of loving, because no matter how you look at it, sex is the one thing he craves. Nature took care of that and created what scientists call a pair bond and most of us call love.

Make Lovemaking Sizzle:

Making love is one thing, but keeping the passion and the excitement turned up makes all the difference. Drive your man madly in love by keeping things sizzling, experimenting with oils, different places and times. Don't fall into a rut of sticking to the same old thing or the same old way. Making love doesn't have to fall on a Friday night or a Tuesday morning. Try a Saturday night and a Wednesday morning. Your regular position may still leave you fulfilled, but another position could add to the excitement. No matter how pleasurable anything is, if you do it over and over, it won't have the same thrill. In other words, the same thing leads to falling into a rut. It leads to boredom. And boredom leads to disinterest; and when disinterest appears in the bedroom, you can kiss his falling in love with you good-bye.

Be & Act Independent:

Be in charge and act in charge of your life. Let him see that you are an independent female. Always be coming or going as if you have a full agenda. Don't sit on the couch waiting for him to ring your phone or knock on your door. Go to the movies, to the shopping mall. Just go. This will make him desperate to catch a minute of your time. And when he comes by for a visit don't bore him with details about your day or friends, your kids, the neighbors. Acting independent will make him feel as if he can never get enough of you. He'll start calling you from work to suggest things to do, planning dates and get together to make sure he's first on your schedule. Men love independent women because they leave them alone. They love chasing women who are busy. It gives them a thrill, as big as a touchdown or a home run.

Give Him Your Attention:

Give your man your undivided attention when you're out together. This is the time to make sure he knows he's your center of attention. If you want to talk and mingle with other friends, make sure to include him. This is the time to put independence on the back burner. Men are very proud when they're out with you; and no matter how easy-going he is, a man is always two seconds from jealousy. They like to have their woman right by their side. Spending too much time with other friends while you're out with him will rub him the wrong way. You don't mean any harm, but he sees it that way. It could produce an argument.

Show Your Appreciation:

It's easy to take appreciation for granted. Just like when we were staying at home, the mother who made us a hot meal everyday and washed our clothes, we didn't say thank you, nearly enough, showing our appreciation because we assumed she's our mother and she should take care of us. But everybody wants to know they're appreciated for what they do, even the mother who loves taking care of her children wants to hear a thank you sometimes. Just as men need to continue doing little things for a woman, she needs to be particularly attentive to appreciate the little things he does for her. With a smile and a thanks she can let him know he has scored a point. A man needs this appreciation and encouragement to continue giving. He needs to feel he can make a difference. Men stop giving when they feel they are being taken for granted. A woman needs to let him know that what he is doing is appreciated. Because men want to be the providers, they want to take credit for a woman's happiness, and they thrive on feeling successful in making a difference. They just need to feel appreciated for it.

Love reaches in and embrace the deepest part of us. the part of us that makes us smile. The part of us that makes us love being able to love. Drive your man madly in love and let the deepest part of your love and his love embrace you both!

Chapter 25

Leave Mothering to His Mother

There probably are not too many of us who can say we haven't crossed that line from time to time from being loving to our mate, to being mothering. A time when we find ourselves treating and talking to the man in our life like he's our child instead of our lover. This kind of treatment may seem harmless, but it can spell the end of your relationship.

And why do we mother our men? Somehow, it's a part of our female makeup. Because "even if a woman is not a mother, the tendency to mother the man in her life grows stronger when she loves him. If she has children, the urge is even stronger. It's difficult for a woman to nurture a man without mothering him," says Dr. John Gray, in his book, *What Your Mother Couldn't Tell You & Your Father Didn't Know*, "When a woman begins to mother a man, she thinks she is being loving and helpful, but she is really sabotaging her relationship."

Your man wants to feel that you trust him to be a provider, and when you mother him, he regards it as your lack of trust in his abilities. By not giving him room to grow and learn on his own, she assumes a responsibility for him, which he gradually begins to resent and rebel against.

In the beginning of a relationship, a woman generally doesn't mother her man. She sees his potential and assumes that he can and will develop and express it. But, over time, as she sees him doing things differently from the way she believes he should, she begins giving him unsolicited advice. She thinks she is helping, but in reality she is sending him the message that he can't succeed on his own. He feels that she is trying to change him. Many women can probably remember moments when they gave their men unasked for advice or responded with motherly concern to something their men did, like Patricia Roberts, a New York City administrative assistant recalls. "I can remember plenty of instances when I not only gave my own boyfriend advice, but men at work, male friends, my brothers and many—a word of advice solicited or unsolicited," laughs Roberts. "I remember once when this co-worker of mine came down to the food truck to get a cup of coffee. It was pretty chilly outside and he had rushed outside without a jacket and was also taking a smoke while he waited. You could see that he was cold because he was shivering. Without any thought, the first thing I did was to ask him, 'Where's your coat, Pete? You're asking for a cold.' That's the kind of stuff women do quite a lot."

Perhaps, Roberts' co-worker didn't mind her expression of concern for his health at that moment, and many men don't, but over time, in a relationship, a behavior pattern is set which eventually erodes the foundation of the relationship, which is really a partnership between two adults who are ultimately responsible for their own behavior and the choices they make.

Admittedly an innate behavior that is encouraged and supported by her traditional upbringing, women's instinctive tendency to mother is difficult to adjust in a love relationship. Nevertheless, for the longevity of the relationship, she must try to find the right combination and temper her concern for her man with a respect and recognition or the reality that he is an adult, not a child.

It is very difficult for a woman with children and/or a career outside the home to shift from the role of mother to the role of lover. Whether or not a woman is actually a mother, the tendency to behave like one is instinctual. for that reason, it is hard for her to discern the differences between nurturing her man with love or mothering him with love. One kind of love is supportive and the other is toxic.

The idea that all men are little boys who need guidance to make the right decisions and not do harm to themselves is a damaging viewpoint which many women are raised to embrace: All men just want to be mothered. They're like babies who need to be appreciated for whatever they do.

This is an unfortunate perception many women have about men, and even though it sounds innocence enough, this attitude is poison to the long-term health of a relationship. A man finds this kind of statement to be completely insulting and demeaning. If a woman continues expressing her love in such a mothering way, her partner would resent her.

Listed below are some classic examples of how some women unknowingly begin to turn a man off by mothering him:

- When a man gets dressed, she says: "I hope you are not going to wear that."

- When a man buys something for himself, she will say: "Did you shop around first? How much did that cost? You paid that?"

- While a man is eating potato chips, she will say: "Those are really bad for your heart. You should not be eating them."

- While a man is working hard to meet a deadline, she says: "If you didn't wait until the last minute, then you wouldn't have to rush like this."

- When a man is driving the car, she says: "You shouldn't drive so fast. You could get a ticket."

- When a man is leaving for a trip, she says: "Do you have your wallet? Do you have your airplane ticket? You didn't give yourself enough time. What if there is a traffic jam, you'll be late."

- When he is fixing the toilet, she says: "You know, if you jiggle the handle, that will help...Maybe you could call the plumber. He will know what to do."

- When a man is in the kitchen making a dish, she says: "I think you should prepare the steak this way. I never prepare it the way you're doing it."

In each of the above examples, the female is preventing her man from making his own decisions by mothering him with unsolicited advice. This kind of advice is not support, and even if he needs some input, he will not hear it.

If you're wondering how and why your man may be offended by unsolicited "motherly" advice, put yourself in his place. For instance, if you are visiting your mother and she says, "It's really cold out there, you better wear your cap and gloves; and be careful driving on those icy streets," it probably really bugs you. That's because she's treating you like a kid instead of an adult. Understand this and you should be able to understand how your man can find it quite insulting.

Next time you get the urge to mother your man, just put yourself in his place and think how you would want to be treated. To appreciate a man for what he does is to nurture his masculinity, and that spells giving him the emotional support that he needs. If you do have a habit of mothering your man, just try and gradually work yourself out of that told pattern. Sometimes old habits are hard to break, but when you are determined and work at them, they get easier and easier to change. Keep in mind that your man is worth it. He will love you for it, and your relationship will only grow stronger!

Sometimes, the best advice you can give your man is no advice at all!

Chapter 26

9 Special Ways to Become His Legend of Love

We all would like to become the legend of one special man's heart. To be that one very out-standing woman that melts his heart. That one person that makes his heart race with just the very mentioning of our name. There's are many ways to become his legend of love, but they all start with the same thing. Making love. His true heart's desire, which means becoming the legend of your man's heart is not an exact science. It's an art at having complete accuracy with fulfilling his desires.

Men are very sexually selfish. Once you realize that you are already ahead of his game. He wants plenty of loving, when he wants it and how he wants it. And it's no mistaking, since the beginning of time, one sure way to keep a man around the house is to fulfill his birthright by keeping his sexual appetite satisfied. So satisfied that his only craving is you. And if you're his every craving, he'll never be on the hunt! You will become his one true love. His legend of love. No matter where he goes or what he does, his thoughts will only focus back to you. Even if you two breakup for any reason. You will always *Become His Legend Of Love*. So I think it would be safe to say, that in order to become his legend of love, keeping heavy appointments with the bedroom, should be at the top of your schedule. Leaving no stone unturned, keeping your relationship sizzling with red hot passionate earthshaking lovemaking.

Lots of Romance:

Along with keeping his sex plate full, throw plenty of romance on the dish. Lower your inhibitions. Be spontaneous. Be silly. Be creative. Being a real romantic is a little like being slightly, enjoyably drunk. It lowers your inhibitions, causes you to act a bit silly sometimes, and gives you the impetus to act impetuous.

Keep the Passion Alive:

Keep the passion alive and always sizzling in your relationship; and never allow this fire to fade out. The way you do this is to change your routine in the bedroom from time to time. One of the chief passion assassins is routine. Even if you are comfortable in your rut, it is helpful to break out of it from time to time. Even doing silly things can help make a moment special and memorable."

Passionate Times Together:

We have already established that the number one rule in becoming his legend of love is giving him plenty of loving. Keeping your sheets sizzling with warm bodies, your and his of course! Making your lovemaking playful and carefree and totally giving of yourself. Because, it's not always how often you make love, it's also how wonderful you make each other feel when you do. The point is to make sex joyful instead of a duty, to make sex loving instead of performing, an occasion for making love instead of just having sex. And when you're feeling wonderful about your passionate times together, your love life will be off limits to boredom. That nasty seven letter word: Boredom. One of the main killers of a relationship. Boredom spells the end of good sex—and often of the relationship. According to one survey, 53 percent of married men think that marital sex is boring. And more than 60 percent of married men have at least one extramarital affair. Max a couple of old sayings, an ounce of prevention is better than locking the barn door after the horse is gone.

Passionate Kisses:

Kissing is the essence of romance, it's hard to keep romance and passion alive without passionate kisses, yet many couples feel they don't need to kiss or they just stop kissing after awhile. But passionate kissing is a very sensuous act that can be very intimate between lovers. "You can make a special event of kissing the whole body, from the head to the toes, covering your partner with kisses. Try kissing hands and palms. One delicious variation is to suck each finger in turn.

Share Your Fantasies:

As long as you feel comfortable with it, try and make one of his fantasies come true and that will surely drive him absolutely wild. "Sharing a fantasy can be the height of intimacy. Fantasies are your most guarded secret and vulnerable thoughts. Fantasy is a chance to play, to indulge yourself and your partner in pleasure. There's an innocence in fantasy, a winning foolishness that dares to be silly or ridiculous. Yet because fantasies are so private, you need trust to share them. You need to enter into and share fantasies cautiously, one step at a time.

Bubble Bath Together:

Taking a warm, soothing sweet smelling bubble bath together will surely make him smile. Being soaped up together is a sensuous, exciting experience. You're in a steamy pleasure boat for teasing and rubbing. Wash each other all over with your hands. You might try a special soap or bubble bath. Giving each other shampoos is fun. You can each take turns being totally pampered by the other. And after the relaxing sweet smelling bath, you can lovingly and carefully towel each other off, kissing every so often as you do.

Passion Over Friendship:

Communicate with him and let him know when something bothers you. Don't keep your feeling inside because you are afraid of hurting his feelings and losing his friendship. Because even though, becoming good friends and staying friends are essential to a lasting relationship, but keeping the passion alive is more essential in order to keep living in love. "Friendship is a breeze if we suppress our feelings. If one partner is willing to sacrifice who he or she is to the relationship, they will always get along—but the passion will die. Once the passion dies, so will his love. Just as it's difficult for a woman to enjoy sex with a man she doesn't love, a man cannot love a woman without feeling sexual toward her.

Your friendship without passion will not keep him. Communicating your feelings to keep your passion alive will. Without good communication skills, quite commonly a couple with a lot of love will choose to maintain the friendship and sacrifice their feelings.

Grow & Change:

In your efforts to become his legend of love, don't deny yourself. Make sure you are being fulfilled and make sure you are continuing to grow with the relationship. Change is automatic if a relationship is to nurture us in being true to ourselves. Just as physical growth is so obvious in our children, we must always continue to grow emotionally, mentally, and spiritually. We must be careful not to sacrifice or deny ourselves too much. When a relationship does not allow us to grow, the passion between two people begins to fade.

Become his legend of love by being willing to change and grow in passion and in love. And even if by chance, your union don't last, you will always remain the one true legend of his heart!

Chapter 27

Acceptance Bonds the Union

Love is the glue that keeps a marriage/relationship together. Acceptance is the strength of that glue that bonds it in terms of whether it will hold or fall apart. Our acceptance of each other happens slowly. After the first rush of love or passion, the irritations show their faces and come out in full bloom.

We are only human and it's hard to accept someone else's faults. It's hard enough to accept our own. But according to Dr. Debora Phillips, author of *Sexual Confidence,* acceptance is granting the people you love their right to be human—their inalienable right to their own flaws. You accept someone because you love them and because you want to share intimacy with that person. You accept their opinions and fears as you accept their eyes and kisses. See how the circle goes: The more you accept me, the more I can accept myself. The more I can accept myself, the more I can risk being vulnerable with you. The more vulnerable I am with you, the more you can trust me. The more we trust each other, the more intimacy we share. The more intimacy we share, the more love we have. And the more I love you, the more I accept you.

Any person at any time can get on that loving train at almost any point. But the easiest way to begin is by being accepting. When you have acceptance in intimacy, you don't need as much praise and approval from the outside world.

If you are accepted in love, you don't have to prove yourself. If you are accepted for who you are and not for who you could be or should be, there's no need for pretenses, or trying to prove how brave, smart, rich, athletic, or sexual you are. Acceptance lets you be yourself.

Knowing you are accepted as you are, and knowing that what you think and feel won't be put down by your lover, gives you the freedom to think and feel more deeply and intensely. You can be irrational, so that what might seem to be weakness to the outside world becomes the shared strength of deep emotion.

With acceptance you begin to feel comfortable taking emotional and sexual risks. When you try something new in sex, there are bound to be mishaps. After all, you are learning. With acceptance, the learning and the adventure can lead to beauty instead of a sense of failure. Acceptance gives you the courage to accept the risk of sexual pitfalls as the price you pay for attempting great leaps.

The art of being accepting, is in taking small, accepting steps, not great leaps. You may have to take hundreds of them. There is so much to accept. It's loving not just their most attractive traits, but also their least attractive ones. After the first highs of romance you begin to notice the refrigerator door has been left open yet again. Dirty clothes and socks are left on the floor. He or she is spending too much money. She takes too long at the grocery store. Suddenly, he drives too fast. Now she doesn't like sex in the morning. He yells too much. She is overprotective of the children. He flirts with your friends. She watches too much television. The list goes on and on. But instead of listing all your lover's faults and adding them up, begin with just one fault and accept it. Try doing it for practice. Just take one small fault and instead of fighting it, instead of letting it drive you up the wall, see if you can relax and accept it. The reason you want to start with something small, something that doesn't bother you much, is that you need to be sure that your love wins out over your annoyance.

Some things are easier to accept than others. Some people don't mind a messy bedroom. Others demand military precision in sheets. Eating habits can be loaded with conflict: He or she fussing that the other is using too much sugar, salt, or fat. So by accepting the small irritations first, the larger areas will diminish in importance.

On the other hand, if you find serious, even destructive areas of conflict—if you find, for example, that your lover is an alcoholic, a compulsive gambler, a constant and severe critic, nonsexual, or, to be less dramatic, can talk only about money—you may also find there is only so much that can be accepted. It may be better to end a destructive relationship than to prolong it.

Chapter 28

Communicating in Lovemaking

This is an area where we could all use a few pointers. Communicating is the key that opens many doors. Without communication we find ourselves running in opposite directions. What good would it do to wait for your husband after work at the corner restaurant, if he has no idea you'll be waiting there for him? Without getting in touch with him and communicating your plans, he would have no idea that you wanted him to meet you.

It would stand to reason that the time to begin communicating in lovemaking is before you begin lovemaking. Of course there is a world of difference between having lived together for thirty years and never having been to bed together. Still, whether it is your first or your five thousandth time together, it is important to say what you mean rather than give vague signals. There are hundreds of ways to ask someone to make love. Some are clearly better than others. Better because they avoid misunderstanding and guesswork. The best, I think, are direct, caring, seductive, and romantic. Here are a few examples that, depending on the circumstances and how you say them, might fulfill all those requirements: "I want to make love with you." "Would you come to bed with me?" "Would you like to make love with me?"

It is important to ask instead of to assume. Assumptions clutter communication. And they are often so inaccurate.

Listen to just a few of the assumptions people make about their partners:

- "She wants to."

- "He doesn't really want me."

- "She's only holding back to tease me."

- "I'm pretty tired and feel crummy. But he wants to, so I guess we will."

- "I know he wants to 'cause he's got that gleam in his eyes."

- "Clean sheets! I guess she wants sex tonight."

- "The way she's kissing me means she wants to go all the way."

The answer to any sexual assumption is "Maybe." And "Maybe not." But after all, why guess? Why not just ask?

No matter how you ask, there's always the chance that you'll be rejected. And since rejection can be painful, I'd like to suggest some ways of making rejection less painful.

No is a strong word. It's not necessarily permanent. You can always change your mind. But there are times when "no" needs to be said: when you are tired, not in the mood, unaroused, afraid of getting pregnant, feeling a lack of intimacy. "Virtually all couples have frequency discrepancies, in which one wants to and the other doesn't," says Dr. Phillips. One wants to once a week, one wants to once a day. No two people are ever in perpetual synchronism in the rise and fall of their sexual desires.

You don't need to have a "good" reason for saying "no." And it is important to say "no" instead of "enduring" sex. Self-sacrifice in sex is not a virtue, it's a form of sexual suicide.

Saying "no" to having sex can be a very assertive and important word to say. Instead of waiting until they feel overwhelmed with desire, many people have sex because they feel pressure to prove their virility, lose their virginity, or simply because they feel they "ought to." (If you don't feel ready for sex, if you don't feel there's intimacy and love, sex can interfere with a relationship and end it before it's had a chance to develop.)

Still, as important as it can be to say "no," how you say it may be even more important.

The problem is that for most couples, "no" sets up a negative pattern. For example, a husband says, "Let's make love, honey." And a wife replies, "No." she feels guilty for saying "no." And he feels cold-shouldered, unappreciated, and rejected. He gets a little angry at that, which makes her angry. So now they're both angry and headed off in separate directions.

When "no" is interpreted as a personal rejection rather than a statement of mood or desire, there are apt to be hurt feelings. Let's look at some ways of saying "no" and of receiving a "no" that are less likely to make a partner feel rejected or angry.

Instead of just saying "no," you can offer a sensual alternative to intercourse:

- "No, but I'd like to kiss you."
- "No, but I'd like to touch you or have you touch me."
- "No, but I'd like to give you a massage."
- "No, but I'd like to give you a back rub."

There are other alternatives.

- "No, but I'd really enjoy lying here with you and talking."
- "No, but it would be nice if we could just read together."
- "No, I really care about you, but I'm just not in the mood."

You can say "I'm not sure." Many times you are not sure, and it's helpful to say so. "I'm not sure" is an especially important alternative for woman. It may increase her "yeses." Many women are so used to taking their sexual cues from men that they don't recognize when they themselves are aroused. Many women don't become aroused before they become involved. So they say "no." But saying "I'm not sure, let's just kiss or a while" leaves time for your feelings to grow or languish until you are sure, one way or the other. You do, however, need to make it clear that saying "maybe" is not a tease—that it is entirely possible that the "maybe" will lead to a "no."

The way you accept a "no" can be just as important as the way you say it. Accept a "no" lovingly and with empathy. Say: "I'm sorry that you're tired." "I am disappointed, because I desire you so much." "I love you. Could I just hold you in my arms as you go to sleep?" Accepting a "no" can be a gesture of love.

Chapter 29

Stay Slim Before and After Marriage

Over and over we are told the same thing, if you want to lose weight, you got to cut back on what and how much you eat, and oh yes, don't forget to exercise. But in many cases, as much as we all know that exercise is something we all need, that essential physical training for our body, which helps us in more ways than we'll ever know, like helping the way all our parts work and function. But, yet with all the good we know we can get from exercising, for one reason or another, we sometimes can't find the motivation or effort to get in to it. It's on that old familiar list: Things I need to start doing; things I keep putting off; things I can't seem to get around to.

And chances are, if you're not already into some kind of exercise routine, you probably have that old familiar list tacked on your refrigerator, held up by two magnets, which stares you in the face everyday. We have the best intentions. But yet again, days and weeks go by and we haven't as much as stood in the mirror and danced. The most exercise we accumulate in a day's time is moving our fingers on the keyboard of our computers. Our fingers are getting lots of exercise, just the parts that gain inches are not.

So, we go on through each day and we never sign up for that health club and if we do sign up, we show up once and by the time we return, we realize that our membership has lapsed. We tell ourselves, there's no time.

For those of us who feel that way, and for those of us who do not, walking is the answer. Yes, walking! It's the easiest exercise ever. It's as simple as breathing. It's an exercise we all can do and enjoy. And it's nothing out of the ordinary. We walk everyday anyway, why not walk for sport and for the enjoyment and reap all the benefits at the same time. You can keep the pounds away before and after the big day by starting your walking routine now. To get started, you don't need to sign up at some club that you won't have time to go time to go to and you won't have to dance for hours to a Jane Fonda or Richard Simmons video! There's only one thing that you'll need to make your routine work, and that's a willing mind.

Lisa, 44, Secretary, from Chicago, was one of those individuals who kept a to-do list tacked on her refrigerator, with exercise at the top of the list. She didn't think she had time for exercise. But Lisa, like so many of us, discovered walking. You can discover walking. I say discover, because we do it everyday, but so many of us just haven't realize that we can do it as a routine and reap all the great health and fitness benefits that walking can do for us.

The wonderful thing about walking is that it's "an exercise for people of all ages and all levels of activity. You can start slowly, set manageable goals, and still derive great benefit from this exercise. Your walking routine can be whatever you feel comfortable with. For better results, your routine should be some kind of casual walking each day. On some days if you feel up to it, after you get comfortable with your walking routine. You can little by little add a little variety. You can do squats, jumping jacks or push-ups against a fence to add that variety to your walk.

Getting yourself situated into a walking routine, you don't have to worry too much about your health condition, or how out of shape you are; chances are, a simple walking routine won't hurt you. But, just to play it safe, if you happen to be someone with a low level of activity or someone who has specific health problems, you should probably check with your doctor before you even start a simple walking routine. But according to the experts, it's very rare case when a patient is told he or she shouldn't walk.

"I was l5 pounds over my regular weight," says Lisa, "and I knew in order to take it off, I needed to do some kind of exercising along with cutting down on my meals, but between six kids, a demanding husband and a part-time job, I never could squeeze in anytime for exercise, and because of that, I never could shake those extra pounds. Then at the end of 1995, while downtown doing some Xmas shopping, I ran into an old friend from a couple years back. I remembered her being heavier back then, but now she was really fit looking.

"I mentioned how she had slimmed down and that's when she told me that she had gotten into walking. That it keeps her looking fit and feeling better. I was impressed and after that talk with Shirley, early that next Sunday morning, I got out of bed while my husband and kids were all sleep, slipped out of the kitchen's door and was on my way. I walked up to the corner 7-11, about two blocks away, then I headed back, taking my time. When I got back home, I discovered, I wasn't even tired. But boy, I really felt good about myself. That started my walking routine. Every morning around 7:00 o'clock I would head on my walking journey and would be back inside in time to see my husband off to work, the kids off to school and then get myself ready for work. It took awhile, some months down the road, but my walking did help me lose some weight!"

Tips To Maximize Your Walking Routine

Keeps the Pounds Away:
Walking works wonders in our efforts toward keeping the pounds away. A survey of over 2,000 people shows they have lost at least 30 pounds and kept it off for a year or more. These people share a commitment to exercise. What kind? Amazingly, 49 in every 50 walk regularly. They do other forms of exercise, too, but walking is the prevalent one. However you drop pounds, walking is usually a key to staying slimmer. It's highly unlikely you'll keep weight off if you don't increase activity. For 95-plus percent of people, that means walking.

It's just so easy, convenient, and easy on the joints, and it burns lots of calories.

30 to 45 Minutes is Key:
How much time should you spend walking? No definitive study has been established saying how many minutes we should walk to get the most out of the walk. But experts say over and over that it's about 45 minutes a day.

Right Shoes:
Don't go walking in those old leather flats that you wear all the time. Wear the right shoes, is what the experts say. So to get the most out of our walk, that's what we got to do. So, if you don't have a pair of walking shoes, before you start on a regular walking routine, you should go out and buy yourself a pair. One of the biggest mistakes people make is walking in running shoes. It's important for a walking shoe to have a beveled heel [the back of the heel is cut so it's angled in, under the shoe] and a stiff heel counter that holds the foot firmly in place as your foot rolls through each step.

A Brisk Stroll:
A brisk stroll doesn't mean you should half run. So you may ask just how fast is a brisk stroll? For most, it should be walking as if you have someplace to go: a level that's not just strolling but not all out of breath, either. Walk at a pace to make your walk enjoyable and before you know it, your walk will be over and you'll be looking forward to your next walk. You'll know you're walking too fast, if you can't seem to hold a smooth conservation with the person you're walking with.

Drink Water:
Treat your walking like any other exercise and make sure you drink plenty of water. Many of us would rather drink anything other than water, so just to remind yourself, sit an empty glass at the sink. Because it's very important that we drink plenty of water when we get into any kind of exercise routine. The experts say, we need to drink at least 16 ounces of water two hours before we walk, then drink 6 to 8 ounces more 20/30 minutes prior.

Watch What You Eat:

Getting in daily walks to help shed off the pounds doesn't mean we can just abandon watching what we eat. If you're not willing to pay any attention to what you eat, you won't lose weight. And explains that as long as we generally eat well, low-fat meals of modest size, eat a variety of nutritious foods, drink plenty of water, walking will do the rest.

Carrying Weights:

Some experts say that we can reap good benefits from carrying weights while we walk, but if you'll thinking like many of us, you're not trying to carry weights and talk yourself out of the walk before you even start. So, it's your choice, but you might want to think twice about doing so, because other than hurting or injuring yourself, says the experts, if you don't properly position the weights, they can make your walking seem more like a hassle. And if you'll like many of us, that's what you're trying to avoid. You want to make it a pleasure, as easy and as simple as possible; therefore, you look forward to it, and you end up sticking to it.

How Fast You'll Lose:

The average 150-pound person walking at a pace of 15 minutes per mile will burn up to 300 calories during a three-mile, 45-minute walk. Some people lose fat but gain muscle. That won't necessarily show up on the scale as losing weight, but the positive changes can be dramatic.

Take a piece of clothing you've had for a while, and see how it fits. That the way to see your progress.

Here's to walking! Staying healthy! And staying slim before and after the big day with the easiest exercise that won't cause you any fuss! Walking!

Chapter 30

How Couples Stay Happily United:
7 Easy Steps for Staying Together

Staying happily united in a loving relationship is what most of us strive for in life. But it's not always what we end up with. Sometimes being a couple can split right down the middle! Burst right at the seams! Why? You didn't work at staying happily united. We work very hard at our careers, and we need to work a little bit harder at our personal lives, keeping love within our grasp. Some of us have been working very hard at careers, but in our personal lives, love and deep intimacy have always remained just a little beyond reach.

We can become workaholics to put ourselves through school, sometimes working two and even three jobs because we are determine to educate ourselves and achieve at our careers and nothing will hold us back. With degree in hand, we get the job of our choice and become a workaholic with just that one position, because we want to be the best at what we do and achieve the highest honors and promotions. We burn the midnight oil, skip meals and other appointments to meet deadlines at all cost, so we can stay on top of our careers. And we let nothing hold us back. But stop and think! Are we that devoted to our personal relationships. Many of us don't always have the same mindset to work at our personal affairs to make sure our relationships remains strong.

In order to stay happily united in your relationship is to understand relationships, to have some better sense of how to make them work. "In the thought system of love, the goal of life is inner peace, and the true purpose of all of our relationships is to join. If we believe in our hearts that when two people come together the real purpose is joining, then certain dynamics are set into motion that can bring peace, harmony, and love into that relationship."

Laugh About It:

Bring a friendly happy medium to the relationship with laughter, smiles and positive thinking. They all serve as an ounce of prevention in keeping your relationship securely in tact. If you are bickering with your mate, if you pause for a second and just laugh about it, he will calm down and laugh about it to. Men are funny that way. They seem to follow our lead. Couples who laugh together and don't focus on negative thinking about their partners, communicate better and stay more warm and loving with each other. Don't fall into a rut of sweating the little things. Just decide you'll no longer allow the little things that annoy you about him to get under your skin. Make a point of doing things together that make you both laugh; look for the humor in the silly things he does—instead of nagging him about them.

Trust is Mandatory:

If for some reason you don't trust your mate and you have no concrete reason to be distrustful, rethink your attitude. Until he gives you a reason to be distrustful. Showing trust and putting your trust in someone is a show of real love. And a showing of real love through trust and honesty is the very backbone of a couple staying happily united. Anything less than trust and honesty will be the death of your relationship. Lies and deceit mounts up to an overbearing load, ripping your relationship right to threads.

Trust means looking past behavior based on fear; it means choosing to see the light of love and the innocence of a child in the eyes of everyone we know or meet in our daily lives. We cannot create positive relationships, ones that are whole and totally loving, until we've healed the unhealed relationships from the past. To learn again how to trust, we need to learn to let go of any emotional investments we still have in our hurtful past.

Acceptance Is Law:

Acceptance of your mate is law if you expect to keep his love and respect. Men are no different from women. We don't want our mates trying to change us, telling us what to wear and how to wear our hair. Same goes for him. If he wants to wear those cut out jeans, let him. It's not worth bickering over. When two people think they can be happily united without accepting each other, trying to change or rearrange each other, they are kidding themselves. Because staying happily united becomes impossible when we can't accept the people we're with for who they are. The most important aspect that reaches to the very essence of our attraction for someone is that we are different. Having to give up who we are to please the one we love ultimately kills our passion and destroys our love. A man feels most turned on and attracted to his partner when she makes him feel like a man. Likewise, a woman is most attracted to a man when he makes her feel totally feminine.

Loving Comments:

Give loving comments for all the loving things he does for you will keep flowers blooming in your garden of united love. Without a sign of appreciation lovers and givers will become disenchanted and stop loving and giving. Just like the worker who wants a pat on the back for the good job she's doing, and the child that wants an acknowledgment for good grades; when we know we're appreciated, it allows us to give and dedicate ourselves more.

Grow Together:

Changing and growing with the time is one sure element you will need to stay happily united. Whatever you do or say, don't let it be something to hinder your mate from changing and growing to the fullest of their potential. And allow yourself to change and grow as well. Because living with the same person, no matter how special or wonderful they are, over a period of time eventually become boring if there is no change and growth. Ever heard anyone say they out grew an old lover? That's means one person changed and moved forward with their life and the other one remained in a rut. This happened to a 24 and 25 year-old couple, Cindy and Will of Chicago, who were once in love. "After we graduated from college, Will found comfort in his mother's home," says Cindy. "Will was pleased to be free of studies and responsibilities, and didn't want to focus on getting a job for awhile," she said, shaking her head. "While he was taking his time about getting a job, I went right out and got one. We grew farther apart until we eventually broke up. The fact that I was moving forward with my life and he wasn't—was a big turn off."

Changing with the pace and keeping fresh is vital to staying happily united. Just as listening to a favorite song a hundred times in a row makes it grow stale, the same goes for couples if they do not grow and change. If husbands and wives do not continue to grow and change, they will surely lose interest in each other.

Kisses & Romance:

Without kisses and romance it's hard to stay happily united. Being happily united is one thing, and being together is another. There are many people who stay together without romance and kisses being apart of their affair. How? They exist in a otherwise normal relationship, but the bedroom door is boarded up and kissing is something that only their pet birds do. They exist in this union for whatever reason (and there is always a big reason when the true essence of love has been abandon), but true happiness is not apart of their union. To survive couple-hood and maintain true happiness with the man you adore, romance, kisses and all the sweet things that go along with it will have to be apart of your relationship: A kiss hello. A kiss good-bye. A passionate kiss just because. Moonlit talks on the front steps. Candlelight dinners. Breakfast in bed. Hot passionate love making behind closed doors. Quiet evenings alone cuddling together and reading each other poetry.

Add Excitement:

Whatever you do, whenever you do it, and wherever you do it, bring some variety into your routine. For instance, if you serve pizza every Friday night, change that night to Wednesday or Thursday. Any relationship needs variety to add spice and newness. Don't allow your love life to become re-runs of the same thing over and over. The same thing can become dull—bringing no excitement or sense of anticipation. Adding variety can be anything from wearing sexy nightwear, to wearing your hair a little different, spending an evening together lying on the living room sofa together to using candles at the bedside will add spice to your relationship—keeping you happily united!

Chapter 31

In-laws: A Package Deal

Walking down the aisle the second or third time gives us a bit of experience in the in-law department. We have been there, done that. We have a good idea of what to expect from our new in-laws. Yet, some of us still have to make adjustment to be able to understand and fit our in-laws into our lives. We forget that some of them just want to fit into our lives and be needed.

Many in-laws expect to treat the new member of the family as just another one of their children, who may be difficult for newcomers to the family who also bring their own set of values.

When the grown son or daughter marries, most of today's parents want a warm and friendly relationship with their child's spouse. Most brides and grooms realize that good relationships with their spouse's parents can make the new marriage and the new future sunnier. How can you, as a new daughter-in-law-to-be make that happen? Read on, and ask your husband-to-be to do the same!

According to Caroline, 58-year-old dry-cleaner worker, "At first I didn't care for my son's new bride. We hardly had a chance to get to know her before the wedding. I had built up my own ideas about her. First of all, she insisted on calling me, Mrs. Barnes after I stressed it would be nice if she called me, Mom like Jimmie. Mrs. Barnes, sounded so formal."

Mrs. Barnes isn't alone in her feeling toward being called by her first name. Your relationship will benefit if you can get up the courage to ask your in-laws if you can call them Mom or Dad. "It isn't disloyal to your own folks and strangely, the couple willing to call their parents-in-law Mom and Dad are more likely to get along better with them than are the couples who continue to refer to them as Mr. and Mrs." You should ask their permission first, but your in-laws should encourage it if they want a warmer relationship. Even Mom Smith or Dad Jones is better than first names and certainly better than waiting until there is an infant so that you can call them Grandpa or Grandma Jones. One of the coldest in-law relationships I have seen was one in which the elderly mother-in-law was always referred to in the third person and never directly addressed by her daughter-in-law.

It wasn't long before I found out that my new daughter-in-law was really a nice woman. She wasn't trying to keep Jimmie away from us. I soon found that out after she kept inviting us over and the two of them dropping by. I love her too death now. By the way, she now calls me "Mom." She had to warm up to me too.

Difficulties with in-laws frequently come from the trouble children have in growing up and away from own parents, and in the reluctance some parents have in letting them do just that.

Fortunately, the fact that people are marrying later than they once did is having a positive effect on this age-old conflict. The groom's mother doesn't feel that the bride has taken away her little boy and probably isn't feeding him right. By the time he marries today, he has been on his own for some time, and if his mother objects to his eating habits, she knows that they are his habits and weren't brought to him by he woman he married. It's more likely that she will be ever so grateful to his bride for bringing vegetables back to his table.

As for the new bride, time was that she could blame all her husband's bad behavior patterns on his mother. Mother didn't teach him to pick up after himself, clean the tub after bathing, replace the cap on the toothpaste. But since he was on his own when she met him, the bride understand that mother's training may have been forgotten and that he irresponsible for his own bad habits. In fact, she may find her mother-in-law an ally in effecting change.

Negative Input/Put-downs:

Studies show that in-law problems occur chiefly at the beginning of a marriage and that disagreements over respective in-laws are most common in the honeymoon stage. So, long before you walk down the aisle or cut the cake, the two of you should promise each other not to blame the other or get caught up in put-downs and negative in-put from either family. Promise each other right from the start that you and your spouse will not blame each other for something your in-laws said or did. Your spouse is not responsible for his or her family's actions. If you are upset, discuss the problem with your in-laws, with both you and your spouse present. And if the relationship continues to be strained, limit the time you spend together.

The negative input by in-laws has been known to make the difference between a successful marriage and one that ends up in divorce court. But if push comes to shove, remind yourself that they were the ones who trained your spouse to make good choices, and you are the good choice. Always be true to your mate!

Accept It:

We all can't have a wonderful mother-in-law like Caroline Barnes, who kept an open mind and realized the beautiful new daughter-in-law she had. It's a fact, some people don't like each other and some of these people are in-laws. If a parent-in-law doesn't approve of the person their grown child has chosen, the time to voice the objections is during the courtship, not after the commitment. If the objections continue, the new bride and groom might consider putting some physical distance between the generations so that only the holidays need to be endured.

Chapter 32

8 Tips to Make Your Marriage a Success

Make your marriage a success, and that will be one of the greatest accomplishments on your life's resume. It sounds easy enough for two people to make their marriage work, after all, in most cases we all want the same thing. No matter how we look at it or think about it, the fact is that underneath all our differences, men and women all want the same things: We want to be loved, cared for, respected and appreciated. We want to know there's a safe place with security and trust, where we can be ourselves, experiment, and grow to our true potential. But as true as those words are, sometimes it's not that easy. We enter into a marriage on top of the world with contentment and excitement of being with the one we love, and some time we can lose sight of the big picture and feel secure with material things: the new house, the car and endless possessions. We can feel that our marriage is a success because of the things we have obtained together. Stop right there! Material things and financial wealth means one thing: you have succeeded in your career and your financial status. On the other hand, your marriage is a whole separate building that stands alone from your career building and your financial building. It's an institution that you have to work on and build from the foundation up. And once everything is in place, you still have to continue the maintenance work to make sure there are no breakdowns. When we are caught up in a false security of thinking our marriage is a success because our career and financial status is a success, we look around in all of our glory at our career and financial tower of success and watch with our own eyes, as our institution of marriage crumbles right down to the ground!

It has been said that the greatest machine on earth came without any book of instructions, referring to the human body. That we somehow manage to get born into this world, and, in spite of environment, we sometimes live a long full life and get to know something valuable. But part of what should to be taught to all of us is how to build up a successful and happy home with the person we marry.

Making a success of your marriage is about many things that have been thrown over into the marriage pot. But, one of the main things happens to be the real attention you give each other and the real time that the two of you spend together. The years will go by and you can either choose to go down one road or the other: You can share your life with your mate or spend your life with your mate. There's a big difference. If you haven't shared your life with that person, you are still together yes, with maybe success in money and career; but suddenly, you are together, but you have grown apart!

Acceptance:

A very important rule in maintaining a lasting union is to be able to be a solid rock of support. In order to be a solid rock of support, accept him as he is or here as she is; because to be totally and completely accepted by the one you love is vital toward maintaining a lasting union. We all want to be accepted for who we are and when we feel like we are not being accepted—something always feel like it's missing from the relationship. One of the most important aspects of attraction is that we are all different; and if we have to give up who we are to please our mate, it pulls away from the love and closeness, which will eventually destroy the foundation of the relationship. But, by putting forth an effort to resolve our differences without having to deny who we are, that helps to secure us of a lasting attraction to each other. One of the quickest ways to push him away is to try to change him—telling him that to be loved and totally accepted by you he has to make a turn around and become someone else…Someone that you can love…Someone that you can accept, since you can't love and accept him as he is. Accepting your mate doesn't mean that you agree with everything he or she thinks or does; rather, you are accepting his or her thoughts and actions as part of the person you love. Many times, after the first highs of romance you begin to notice little simple things that shouldn't even raise an eyebrow, but it does. And you start to fuss and explain about the smallest things. The fact that someone forget to pick up milk turns into name calling and sudden he/she isn't talking to each other. Why? A simple little thing like forgetting to pick up milk surely didn't cause that big fight, but a simple thing like not being accepting of each other surely can. It's quite simple to be accepting; it means learning to live with the next person's shortcoming; it means giving your mate understanding instead of criticism.

Romance:

Romance is very important to stay on track toward a lasting union. Keep it on your agenda no matter how heavy your workload, or how many other obligations you may have; just flat out make time for the romance. Try sneaking it or squeezing it into every aspect of your everyday life together. For instances, if you have kids, leave them with your parents or the sitter sometimes and spend romantic evenings alone listening and dancing to your favorite music; enjoy a romantic meal by candle light, take a stroll in the moonlight. You can turn everyday events into little celebrations; opportunities to express your love for your partner. We're not talking passion here, but affection. A tiny bit of forethought can turn the ordinary into the special. Eat dinner by candlelight. Tie a ribbon around a cup of bedtime tea or coffee. Pop your own popcorn while watching a video at home. Turn his or her birthday into a birthday month! Celebrate that person's birthday every evening. According to America's Romance Coach, Gregory J.P. Godek, author of *1001 Ways to Be Romantic*, "Romance is an art, not a science: You can't predict it or get it perfectly. Romantics often work long and hard to pull off some of their romantic masterpieces. Romantics plan and scheme, buy gifts ahead-of-time, search for sales, and stock-up on greeting cards."

Be Friends:

Sweet romance attracts that special someone to you like glue. The friendship holds them there. Romance is the perfume and spice of intimacy; friendship is the cement. Couples rarely stay lovers without friendship. So, pulling out all the stops to be best friends with your mate is essential to a successful marriage. You may ask yourself, why do I need this person to be my friend? I just need this person to be my lover and my companion. Well, think again. Because if you expect to stay happily united, you will need your mate to be your friend. The friendship between the two of you will work as a cushion that will protect your relationship when it comes back down to earth and falls off those first extremely high peaks of early romance. If there is a strong bond of friendship between the two of you, you can accept the downs when they roll in like thunder.

An example: Sally married Walter, but they never developed a friend-ship with each other. When Sally went through a rough time over her parents' death, Walter didn't want to hold her hand, listen to her talk about them or give her a shoulder to cry on. He couldn't be a friend to her, something she needed most of all, because he wasn't her friend. Sally divorced Walter after she got her strength back. Keep in mind, that the very precious friendship that the two of you develop will be the thing that will keep you connected. Just like the saying, a man's best friend is his dog. And why is that? It's because a dog gives his owner unconditional love and doesn't put down or call his owner nasty names—regardless of what his owner says or does. The same kind of unconditional love and kindness that a person gets from his or her dog, is the same kind of kindness and consideration he or she wants from a mate. We all want that special person in our lives to be a friend who will lift us up and make us feel good about ourselves. Friendship is an effective antidote to the impossible expectations of the Cinderella myth: Somewhere out there someone perfect waits for me. Friendship helps us to accept and love Cinderella even when she's no longer the belle of the ball. Friendship helps us accept/love Prince Charming when he has given up his throne. What is being a friend? Friendship is being there when you are needed, helping to fight each other's battles, and soothing each other's pains and disappointments. Friendship is giving kind words to your mate about his or her strengths, instead of criticizing his or her weaknesses. The friendship we share in our relationships is the nonsexual side of intimacy—sharing our hopes, plans, dreams, and frustrations.

Trust:

Entering into a marriage is like walking with a blindfold on, it all boils down to trust; and in a lasting, meaningful union—trusting each other should come as easy as breathing. If it doesn't, it's like a constant fight against itself. In a case where there's no trust, what's the point of even trying to make it work. But often times in a relationship, many of us feel "the hell with trusting him," because it just isn't in the cards, it seems. But think again! Focus on your bottom line: your marriage is a lifetime commitment. And to make your marriage a success, trust has to be a part of the package. According to Webster's new world dictionary, the definition of trust is "A firm belief in another's honesty, reliability." This means, if he goes out with the guys for the evening, you won't ask too many questions or get upset. And if he happens to get home late from work sometimes you won't get upset; because, frankly, if you don't trust him, he will know it. Once he senses mistrust, automatically his heart locks, keeping it clear of lasting love. When our attitude is open and receptive toward our spouse, a man feels trusted. To trust a man is to believe that he is doing his best and that he wants the best for his partner. The secret to growing in trust is not to expect your man to be perfect. Try to understand how men are different; and enable yourself to trust that he loves you even when he doesn't instinctively do the things you would do to demonstrate caring.

Focus:

Whether you have a roaming eye or not, is not the point. You know you don't have a roaming eye, but the point is, if he thinks you have a roaming eye—do all you can to make sure he doesn't think you do. By nature, men seem to be more toward the jealous side and can easily feel uncomfortable if their mate seems too friendly with other men. The other guy can be an old friend or just a co-worker, but your man will still feel a tinge of jealousy. Give him no reason to feel that tinge of jealousy. When the two of you go out and about, give him ninety five percent of your undivided attention for the whole time you're out. It's okay to talk or mingle with friends that you run into, just don't leave him alone for too long while you do so. Your friends realize you're out with your husband, and they don't expect you to give them too much of your time just because you happened to have bumped into them. Doing so, is a big turn off to a man, and it could prove to be stepping off the track of a successful marriage!

Listen:

Men are not that different from us. Some time they just want us to listen while they get certain things off of their chest. Maybe he had a bad day at work and just wants to talk about it. Don't volunteer any advice unless he asks for it. Try to lend your ear even when he's ranting and raving about something as well. It's not always easy to know what to do when your mate gets upset. One of the hardest things for many women is to be quiet and listen to an angry man. If he's angry, chances are, we're angry too. Though, we all know that arguments and heated discussions can run a loving relationship right into the ground, we want to keep from bickering, until he stops. We should just listen and let him get whatever it is off of his chest; and once he has calmed down, then we can explain our side. According to Dr. John Gray, author of *What Your Mother Couldn't Tell You & Your Father Didn't Know*, "When a man talks while angry, he is generally heavily invested in being right. Sometimes when a man is angry, a woman should take special pains to postpone conversation."

Talk:

It's vital to keep the lines of communication open, letting each other know how you feel and what you're thinking. Above all else, if the lines of communication come to a brick wall, your relationship won't have much ground to stand on. Having heart-to-hearts and opening up to each other helps couples stay close. If something your partner does bothers you, talk to him and encourage him to do the same. Set aside some time to be alone together to have more intimate conversations. Just bear in mind, how good open talks and serious communication in a relationship are similar to a solid foundation in a house. If a house is built with a strong foundation, it will be able to withstand the stress caused by natural disasters. Even if the rest of the house is damaged or destroyed, if the foundation is solid the house can be rebuilt.

Soften Attitude:

We all get heated under the collar and get the urge to fuss, nag and complain. It's never pretty, and over time it can wear holes in the leather of your relationship. It's been said that a tiger can't change his stripes, but maybe he can change his attitude; try being totally positive, accepting, supportive and non-judgmental for three to four days in a row with no nagging, complaining, or heated discussions. It could make a world of difference in strengthening your bond and making your marriage last a lifetime.

If you want to be a cook in some of the best restaurants, you go to chef school. And if you want to be a professional dancer you take lessons. If you want a degree, you go to college to get a job as a teacher, lawyer, or engineer, to name a few. And not one of those jobs mentioned are as important or as difficult to handle as the job of making a success of your marriage. Yet when many of us walk down the aisle with the men of our dreams, we just say our "I dos" and hope for the best. Don't just hope for the best for your marriage, give it your best and make your marriage a success!!

Chapter 33

Make Your Marriage Last a Lifetime

No matter how good the relationship, the passion always makes it better. The passion is like a huge flame that radiates the heat and keeps things sizzling in your love life. But you have to keep in mind and remember this one solid fact: your passion flame can only keep burning if you feed the fire. It won't stay on auto drive forever. During a new marriage or love relationship, passion burns at full speed. But after awhile the flame starts to simmer to a low fire. This is the time it will require some effort from both parties.

And as surely as the sun will rise tomorrow, the sweet spice of your relationship, which is that thing called passion, will surely die if you don't nurture it along the way. It's as simple as this, a lasting, loving relationship cannot survive without passion. And when we love deeply and care so much, letting passion die is the most insidious mistake of them all because it is usually the product of something cold or heartless we said to the other person, an apology we neglected to give, a very important word we forgot to say, or something that we never learned how to do. When you are deeply in love and you wake up to find that the passion is zero, you wonder what happened to your beautiful connection.

7 Simple Ways to a Lasting Love:

Communicate Your Feelings:

Regardless of how much of an attitude you may have with your man about something he said or did, don't give him the silent treatment and keep negative feelings bottled up inside of you about him. It won't fix the problem. Instead, do all you can do to get what is bothering you off your chest. Communicate with him about how you're feeling and try to clear the air. Don't be one of those who fall into a rut of just keeping quiet and allowing the passion to take a trip from your relationship, because the mistake of letting passion die begins with a breakdown in communication. When you choose not to confront your mate about your anger, hurt, and disappointment, the emotions do not magically disappear. Instead, they build a wall between the two of you. Until that wall comes down, you will not feel the good feelings you need to desire your mate sexually. If you asked any couple who have allowed the passion to die out of their relationship they would probably say that the wall between them rose slowly, almost imperceptibly, as one small hurt was matched by another and another until one day they simply could not reach around the wall.

Acceptance & Understanding:

Being understood and accepted for who we are is what we all want from that special person in our lives. What it boils down to is that if you can accept just one small flaw as a part of the person you love, your love will grow that one step. Acceptance leads to vulnerability. You have to feel you will be accepted, you have to trust your partner, before you can expose the vulnerable sides of yourself. We don't want to be made over or given the feeling that we must or need to change in order to deserve their love. It's not that much different from when we were growing up, we all hoped to get acceptance and understanding from our parents, and we felt better about ourselves when we knew we had their understanding and acceptance. It's the same thing for two people in a relationship, because if we have to give up who we are to please our partners, that alone would ultimately kill the passion. If we can somehow place our cards on the table and find that middle ground to resolve our differences without having to deny our true selves, then we can be absolutely sure to find a lasting attraction between each other.

Trust & Honesty:

The backbone of a strong passionate marriage is honesty. Honesty is the cement of the foundation. It's the glue that holds your foundation firmly. The whole idea of building a solid foundation starts with just telling the simple truth. Without honesty, there's no trust; without trust, there's no respect; without respect, there's no love; without love, there's no real hold on your man. In a number of articles I have read the same message: that one of the major secrets to growing trust in any marriage or relationship is not to expect your mate to be perfect. The key is for couples to try to understand how each individual is unique and different in their own way. We should try to trust that the special person in our lives loves us, even when he or she doesn't do or say the things we would do or say in a similar situation.

Togetherness:

Find time for togetherness; going places and doing things with each other is the fuel that helps to keep a couple's passion flame ablaze. It's easy to fall into a rut of thinking we can have that long talk, that romantic candle-lit dinner, that special time alone later or some other time. But after feeling too comfortable in a marriage or relationship, that time never seems to come, due to other pressing things that seem to end up on the front burner. You have a thousand excuses and thousand more things to do; but on a scale of one to ten just ask yourself how many of them rank as high as your marriage or love relationship. So, regardless to what that something may be, always aim for quality time together; and just do it in spite of your schedule and lifestyles.

Time for Loving:

Above all, no matter how much you love each other or want to keep your passion alive, it will never survive if you don't put forth the effort to find time for loving. Regardless of your schedule or his schedule, you have to make appointments with the bedroom a priority. Even though, you may have the kids to tend to, or meals to make or people to visit or things to do, and you just find yourself overwhelmed by so many demands that are pulling you in every direction, the bottom line is quite clear: you are the one who decides who and what will take up your time, your energy, and your affection. Just as easily as you promised your friend, Susan that you would stop over and play cards, you can choose to do something special with your mate. You have the choice to make your marriage or love relationship a priority. But you've got to really want to.

Communicate Sexual Desires:

There are many women who feel if they speak up in the bedroom it might make their partner feel uneasy...as if he's not pleasing them. But if you don't speak up you're not being fair to yourself or your mate. Those of us who allow ourselves to be selfish in bed, have far better sexual experiences. One of the biggest complaints any mate could have, is not knowing what their partner needs and wants from them in bed. For example, one of the lovemaking tools that keeps passion alive is when couples touch each other. But sometimes the way your partner touches you sexually may not be 100 percent to your satisfaction. That's why letting each other know what you want in bed is so important, because when inhibitions prevent you from explaining your needs to each other, sexual touching could even become negative in your mind, making the two of you want to bypass the touching and head straight into making love. But without loving touches, you'll soon look around and find the passion has packed up and moved out of your marriage/relationship.

Support & Appreciation:

Showing your support and appreciation of each other will play a big part in fueling the romantic fire in your relationship. This step is pretty simple, because all it takes is a big kiss for that new gift, or a thank you for the nice dinner out, or a big hug for that single rose or bouquet of flowers. As women, we feel romanced by the beautiful flowers, the boxes of candy and anything from a jewelry store; but on the other hand, a man feels romanced by a woman's appreciation of him. When he does little things for you and you show your appreciation, that makes him feel romantic.

We can make our marriage and the passion that holds us together last a lifetime just as long as we remember not to forget, that the passion in our relationship is similar to growing a delicate rose. A gentle rose is subtle and beautiful, but its beauty is as fragile as a bubble in the wind. It needs nurturing and care to continue to radiate its radiance.

Chapter 34

Recapture Your Spouse's Affection

In every marriage there are days when the bright sunny days fades into the clouds and a little rain will fall. We don't mean to, but these gray skies appear when we unintentionally drive our relationships into the ground with our negative attitudes and fussy ways. We fall into a rut of nagging and bickering with our partner about the smallest things. We are somehow not able to put ourselves in his shoes and look back at ourselves to realize how nerve-wrecking our constant bickering must be to him, until the morning we wake up and notice a huge ice cube sitting on his shoulder. All the ice water we have thrown his way about this little thing and that little thing has finally accumulated to a huge iceberg, replacing his sweet, loving side. When this happens, we come face to face with the cold hard facts that our negative attitude and constant nagging has driven a wedge between our closeness. Many times when this happens between couples, the distance is too far to reach, breaking the thread that bonds you both before you can somehow mend the gap.

There are many things that can cause your husband to start giving you the cold shoulder, but instead of jumping the gun—thinking it's because of another woman or because he doesn't find you appealing anymore, stop and think for a moment if you could possibly fall into the category of being a nag or too fussy. And of course, nobody likes to think of themselves in that way, but just ask yourself one question,

Recapture Your Spouse's Affection

"Am I on his back constantly about things that could really be overlooked?"

5 Signs That He's Giving You the Cold Shoulder:

- **The Silent Treatment**: Has your mate started giving you the silent treatment, asking and answering only necessary questions with little or no small talk in between.

- **He's Pulling Away**: Has he started pulling away and staying his distance from you (if you're in a room he tries not to enter it)—spending more time away from home, finding things on the outside of your relationship that ties up most of his time, not interested in any of your suggestions to go places or do things together?

- **Mealtime Silence**: Do you find yourself doing all the talking during your meals together and he just nods and hardly responds at all, if any?

- **No Attention/Affection**: You can't get his attention or affection no matter what. Even putting on your best dress and buying the sexiest nightwear doesn't seem to get him to look twice at you lately?

- **He's Not in the Mood**: Is he turning his back to you in bed when he is the one who is usually always in the mood?

If you can answer yes to at least two of the mentioned questions, it's possible that your husband is giving you the cold shoulder and you need to recapture his affection. A man will start pulling away and eventually stop feeling desire for a negative woman. Are you guilty of fussing and nagging at him more than usual and being more negative than positive? Have you somehow strayed away from that loving way you used to be with him? If this rings true for your relationship, he has most likely pulled away and is showing less interest because of your negativeness. And since he is still around despite the negativeness, that proves that he still loves you as much as before, but has found a safe haven by staying at arms length of you, trying to avoid all the shouting and agitation that your togetherness brings.

5 Ways To Recapture His Affection:

Understanding:

Understanding is the key to recapturing your spouse's affection. People say and do certain things for certain reasons and to keep your relationship moving smoothly, you need to try a bit more under-standing with your mate. Understanding that he is not trying to neglect or hurt you or leave you out, just because he wants to spend some time by himself or with his buddies. Put yourself in his shoes, you want to do the same—spend some time alone and with your friends, and by doing so you don't love him any less. Understand the same applies to him. Just because he wants to spend some time alone or away from you doesn't mean he loves you any less. A man by nature needs to feel free to roam, and he can go to the ends of the earth, only to return to you. But just like a caged animal, he won't feel free to show you his loving side if he feels trapped. So if you try to understand your husband a little bit better you'll be able to accept them more.

Encouragement:

Traditionally men are considered the breadwinners and the head of the household in terms of making decisions for the entire family, but men seem to depend heavily on their woman's suggestion to validate their own. For example, if you're shopping together and he spots a shirt he likes and says, "I think I would look pretty good in this." And you remark, "I don't think so." Most likely he would agree with you and not bother spending his money on it. So by encouraging him to do some of the things you know he enjoys doing: pool, bowling, card games and etc. (that you have fussed about in the past) will make him feel warm toward you from your thoughtfulness and consideration. And if he's feeling cozy and warm toward you while out with his hobbies, he'll surely feel warm toward you when he gets home, being encouraged to cuddle up in bed and give you that loving side of him.

Tenderness:

Try more tenderness with your mate—giving him lots of hugs and kisses on every chance that you can. Listen closely and pay close attention and you'll find that your husband responds lovingly toward your good mood and your tenderness. A man receives love differently from a woman. Her good mood makes him feel loved. Even when she enjoys the weather, a part of him takes the credit. A man is happiest when a woman is fulfilled. And if you're being pouty and in a bad mood all the time, he can't be happy because he doesn't think you are. A man will react to our actions. When we say kind words and show our loving side they will do the same. So recapture his affection by making a solid effort to be more sweet and loving toward him, the way you used to be back when you first started dating. You would drive from one side of town just to be with him, and you would compliment him and make him feel loved and wanted. You were always on your best behavior because you wanted to make him happy, and by making him happy that's how you won his love.

Avoid Criticism:

This is where the mess hits the fan. If it's one thing men cannot stomach, it's being told what to do and how to do it. Listen to him with a gentle ear and try to avoid being too critical about every little thing he does or says. Unsolicited advice is generally taken as criticism to a man. The point is to be your spouse best friend. And good friends don't criticize each other and make each other feel bad. That's why good friends seek each other out and talk over their problems. And that's one of the main reasons good friends like being around each other. Besides, nobody likes to be criticized, especially for bad habits that are not always that easy to break, such as smoking. Saying things like, "You must be silly to keep putting that pollution in your lungs," are not friendly words. So be your warmest and nicest toward him when the two of you are holding a conversation, and by talking to him in a more loving way without all the fussing and pouting, he'll look forward to holding conversations with you again.

Lovemaking:

One of the most important things you can do toward recapturing his affection is to make sure you share intimacy and add lovemaking to the top of your agenda. If in the past, you have constantly told him that you're not in the mood or you're too tired and beat or maybe you have just turned your back to him repeatedly, without even giving him a kiss good night, you could rekindle his desire by initiating love-making and he'll be encouraged, breaking him out of that 'lost interest stage. Sexual gratification is important to a man. He needs constant reassurance that his partner likes sex with him. Sexual rejection is traumatic to a man's sense of self. When a man is repeatedly rejected, he will suddenly lose interest in sex with his partner.

It's pretty easy to regain that loving side of him. Just be your sweet loving self and give him that smile and that kiss and that hug that you used to. And this has got to be the oldest saying around, but it works and it's true: The thing it took to get him—will be the same thing that will keep him!

Chapter 35

8 Ways to Cultivate Sex Appeal and Keep the Passion Sizzling

Passion ignites the flame that keeps the home fire burning. If the home fires are burning, the warmth will generate throughout the relationship. Passion is true to its form. If the passion is being fed and appointments with the bedroom are being kept, it will bond togetherness and hold down tension and stress in your relationship. Down through generations of man and woman, no matter how good the relationship, the passion always makes it better. The passion is like a huge flame that radiates the heat and keep things sizzling in your love life. You keep in mind and remember this one solid fact: your passion flame can only keep burning if you feed the fire. It won't stay on auto drive forever. During a new and exciting affair, passion is at full bloom, burning at full speed and you don't have to add fuel to the fire. But after awhile the flame starts to fade.

To keep the passion sizzling, now and forever in your marriage/relationship you have to take control of yourself and cultivate sex appeal every chance you can. You cannot turn back the hands of time and be exactly who you were when the two of you first met. But you can commit yourself to taking responsibility for keeping yourself and your life vibrant, interesting, and exciting. when we do things to make ourselves happy—including everything from pursuing hobbies to masturbating when he's not available or interested—we don't resent our mate for failing to make us happy.

Admit that you have allowed work, the kids, the house, the world, to come between you and your mate, and you must vow to steal back some private time for the two of you. When you feel you must choose between spending an afternoon doing something around the house or sneaking out for a quiet, romantic picnic, vow to be "bad." After all, what's the worst thing that could happen? Or as you might prefer to think of it, the best?

To feel and be sexually attractive, you must think of sexual attractiveness as a full-time state of mind, not just an attitude you put on in bed, then toss back into the closet.

A friend named Janice, who is the wife of a good friend, named Otis, told me that her new husband, Otis, just didn't seem interested in sexual relations anymore. "The first four months of our marriage I had no complaints, everything was just the way it should be. Now all he does is give me a kiss good night and turn his back." I talked to Otis and he explained to me in so many words that Janice just didn't turn him on anymore. "I still loved her and miss the romance that used to be between us. But she just lets herself go now. She works out of the house as a freelance manuscript typist, so when I leave for work she is dressed in a robe and when I get home she's dressed in the same robe. It's a turn-off."

Don't fall into Janice and Otis's rut. Make a point of getting the passion in your relationship alive by cultivating sex appeal—in or out of bed:

A Few Ways To Keep Passion Sizzling

- Determine your most special or unique feature, and play it up. Choose clothes that show off your figure, jewelry that accents your hands or your face, shoes that give you that walk, and makeup and/or hair color—even if it's subtle—that give you that extra sparkle.

- Practice walking with confidence and pride: shoulders back, chest out, and eyes straight ahead. Look as if you know where you're going & how to get there. If you don't feel it, fake it until you do.

- When you're with friends, show that you're glad to see them. Laugh and have a good time. It's a turn-on.

- Whether you home in-home or outside the home, make a point of getting up every morning and getting dressed as if you did work outside. "Take care of yourself. Whether your style is a natural, well-groomed look or something more elaborate and sophisticated, always look your best. It tells everyone, "I care about myself.

- Be confidence and proud of yourself. Work with what you have. "Don't let having a cold, an outbreak of blemishes, or a few extra pounds diminish your confidence or your sexual power.

- Always be yourself. When you're talking to your mate, be as real, honest, direct, and expressive as you would be with your same-sex friends.

- Cultivate a good sense of humor. Learn to loosen up and laugh at yourself and at life. Humor is a turn-on because it keeps life's problems in perspective.

- Finally, don't fall into a bedroom rut: Try to bring some variety behind your closed doors. Variety keeps boredom out. Boredom is one of the biggest problem men have with their wives. You may know your favorite pie is blueberry—has been, always will be. But most likely, you do not limit yourself and never try a slice of lemon or apple? And so it is with making love, why limit yourself to the same routine? Doing so can throw your relationship into a rut. The woman who puts on her face cream and wears the same nightie every night and does the same routine in the same room at the same time is asking for trouble. Use imagination and give him some variety.

Take a stand to protect your relationship and cultivate sex appeal into your relationship. Don't let that love destroyer "boredom" creep into your affair. When you ignore the passion by thinking it can sizzle on its own, is the very instance, you throw your passion out of the window to survive on its own. And on its own it will without a doubt fade to black. Maybe you are thinking that it has already faded to black. No appointments in the bedroom for weeks at a time. If that's the case in your relationship and you feel too much water is under the bridge and there's just no going back to being passionate with your mate. Remember, you and your mate were sexually attracted to each other long before the first kiss or that first special night. You were turned on by the total person, by how he treated others as well as by how he treated you and how he felt about himself. So before you throw the idea of keeping the passion burning in your relationship out of the window, think about the suggestions: hot lingerie and silk sheets may work wonders.

Chapter 36

20 Secrets to Lasting Trust

When you think of lasting trust, the word "openness" may come to mind: Openness with yourself and your thoughts. And the word vulnerability may come to mind because to open yourself up will leave you vulnerable. Vulnerability means exposing all the sides of yourself. That means taking real risks. The reward of vulnerability is more love and trust. The more you close off, the more invulnerable you are and the less you will feel. On the other hand, the more you disclose of yourself, the more intensely you will be able to feel. This is where the risk and reward become tangled together. For in being open and vulnerable you are laying yourself open to pain as well as to love. But that's the name of the game. To receive love and trust and maintain lasting trust in your relationship, you have to have an open heart on both ends: Giving and receiving.

Consistency:

You can trust what is evident; you don't have to worry about hidden agendas. You don't have to feel as if you need a private detective, or need to be one, to find out what is really going on.

Reliability:

Reliability and dependability, dependence and reliance develop over time. For example, your partner calls when promised or takes care of the bills each month as agreed. More important, you have learned you can depend on your partner in situations where you could feel hurt or rejected if let down. Without reliability, relationships can deteriorate.

Agreements:

Keeping agreements. Trust is definitely strengthened when your partner's promises are fulfilled. Conversely, a failure to keep promises erodes trust. Credibility is shattered. The process of trusting becomes a lottery, where you start asking, will it pay off this time or not?

Being Honest:

A major trust builder is knowing you can count on your partner's statements to be true and not misleading. This means you expect your partner to be truthful, but also to be complete. Leaving out important information is a lie of omission. Slick, evasive statements leave you standing on ever-shifting sand. If you start feeling you can't trust what your partner is saying then you need to discuss this.

Being Open:

Being emotionally open and receptive. Given emotional support and understanding, we expose more of ourselves. Sharing, when combined with our partner's willingness to be self-disclosing, is the key to intimacy. Conversely, when emotional receptivity isn't present, we may hold back. We may even find conversation diminishing to brief exchanges. And if you experience long periods of silence, that's a warning sign—something is seriously wrong.

Feeling Understood:

Most of us want a partner who not only listens but also shows understanding. Over time, you expect your partner to know your views on important issues as well. Otherwise, the fire of love and passion may become dampened by resentment. Your anger is likely to be the result of feeling that you are not important enough to him.

Having Empathy:

When feelings are identified and expressed in an empathic manner, a couple will sometimes find that the real difficulty has little to do with what they are arguing about. A fight about flirting at social gatherings, for instance, might only be a symptom of assumptions: "If you loved me, you wouldn't do this" or "If you respected me, you'd trust me." The fears behind the Assumptions are quite similar: "I'm afraid you don't love me/trust me." The surface disagreement may express the differences in the way each partner avoids or copes with similar feelings. Only via empathy will a couple achieve a level of discussion in which these discoveries will occur.

Sharing Confidences:

When you trust, you can share personal views with your partner, both small everyday matters and larger revelations. It is comforting to know that your partner is willing not only to listen but also to safeguard your disclosures. It's especially important to feel you can trust your partner to maintain confidentiality.

Feeling Safe:

Feeling safe during disagreements. Those who try too hard to deny disagreements, or are afraid to bring them up, end up with a shell of a relationship. On the other hand, for some couples, bringing up sensitive issues produces an explosion. It can lead to wounded feelings and even wounded people. As a result, couples may move further apart.

Disagreements:

Resolving disagreements. Confidence in resolving disagreements. The German philosopher Arthur Schopenhauer told the story of two porcupines huddled together on a cold winter's night. Each kept getting pricked by the other's quills. Finally, with much shifting and shuffling, they managed to work out an equilibrium. Many couples have much in common with these huddling porcupines. They want to achieve warmth and closeness but also want to avoid getting jabbed.

Sharing Information:

Openness in sharing information. Being in a relationship, some contend, affords them the privilege of being less diligent in their efforts to communicate. In effect, they say, "You ought to know how I feel or what I mean if you really love me." Unfortunately, most people do not read minds.

Sincere & Genuine:

Being sincere and genuine. Imagine that you are at a park, listening to an attractive person—and you're beginning to fidget. It's not that you're bored. He is charming and so smooth that you check your valuables to make sure they're still there. That is the kind of impression some people make. They seem to know just what to say at the right time, yet they don't feel quite sincere, like the glib politician or persuasive salesperson.

When You're Apart:

Trusting your Partner when you're apart. If you feel anxious about your partner's outside activities, maybe your partner has really done something to merit mistrust. But consider whether you are perhaps being overly sensitive because of your own doubts. Doubts can come from many sources. For instances, when your partner does something without you, do you feel abandoned or neglected? Do you interpret that need for time alone as a rejection? Do you fear your partner may be saying: "I don't like being with you anymore?"

Extended Absences:

Trusting your partner during extended absences. Perhaps your partner has to travel extensively for work. Or perhaps one of you wants to go on a vacation and the other can't, or doesn't want to. When time apart becomes extended, fear about abandonment, being neglected and rejection may surface. The feeling may be more intense than in brief separation because of the longer absence.

Believing Your Partner:

Believing your partner has your well-being at heart. An active concern for the growth and satisfaction of a love partner means that the concerned individual thinks about and does things to promote the other's well-being. Behaviors viewed as supportive may, of course, vary from person to person.

Personal Responsibility:

Taking personal responsibility when things aren't satisfactory, both partners know who's at fault. Just ask them—it's the other person! In order to right things, all that remains [as far as each spouse is concerned] is enlightenment; that is, for the other person to see the light, confess being at fault and atone. It never works. In fact, when we assign responsibility for our malaise to another person, we impede our own change energy and become a victim.

Feeling Rejection:

If your partner regularly rejects your feelings, thoughts and actions, you will almost surely feel diminished and alienated. You may find yourself preoccupied with protecting and defending yourself; in time you'll probably begin to withhold when you think your partner will disagree. You will then communicate less and may grow apart.

Desiring Sex:

While there's no ready formula for connecting sexually, being able to relax and enjoy each other certainly helps. In order to do this, a couple has to go beyond the physical experience; without the intimate exchange of thoughts, feelings and desires, even the most fiery of sexual relationship will soon dry up.

Handling Money:

Handling money fairly and openly: Money, like sex, is another area of great sensitivity. Surrounded by loads of expectations, it is part of an exchange based on giving or taking away power. Sometimes the person who controls the money views it as a source of power and prestige, while the other partner feels put down, diminished and controlled. By contrast, when money matters are shared and discussed openly, the relationship is more egalitarian.

Loyalty & Confidence:

Feelings of loyalty and confidence in the future. Finally, if we feel encouraged, we feel loyal and committed to our partner. We are willing to put in the energy and effort because we are making a long-term investment. Of course, none of us can predict the future nor be certain that love will endure. But we do need a reasonable sense of basic stability. The promise of continued togetherness enhances a feeling of safety.

Chapter 37

70 Ways to Love Your Lover

There are more ways than you can imagine to love your lover, but no matter how many ways you can think of, they all should begin and end with romance and passion! Your efforts and his to ignite each other's fires and fulfill each other's desires. The hotter your routine the better. Couples will walk away from a fading relationship without hesitation once the passion dies. We want a lifetime of love; we want lasting passion.

- **Romantic Prepared:** Romance in your sex life is like the strawberries in ice cream. It just makes it that much better. We should be prepared to create the proper ambiance for romance. Not only do you need great romantic background music, you need a way to play it non-stop for several hours. Get a tape player with auto-reverse; or get a CD player with slots for three or more discs. Nothing breaks the mood like getting up in the middle of a romantic meal, intimate discussion or lovemaking session, to run over to the stereo. Be prepared to move straight into cuddling and sleeping after lovemaking. If you wear contact lenses, trade your regular lenses for extended wear lenses. So you won't have to break the mood after lovemaking to get up and wash, rinse and disinfect those lenses.

- **Pull It Off:** Even if you've been living together for a while and even if you're going to bed together after a long, hard day, and want to take a bath to get refreshed and comfortable—even then it's sometimes nice to bathe and then get dressed again so that undressing can be part of your lovemaking. There are many ways to undress to heighten the rising passion. Take your time. The longer it takes you to slip out of those Levi's and work them down your body—the more ready you will make him, anticipating what's coming his way. You can take off your things, one at a time, slowly, while he watches. Or you can fan the flame just as much if you take off his clothes slowly, with a lot of kissing and caressing along the way with each zipper you undo or each button you unbutton. In any case, don't just throw off your clothes and hit the sheets. Leave some things on to be taken off.

- **Place An Ad:** Place a personal ad to that special man in your life and list it in your local newspaper under the personal column. Let your man know why he is so special. This will not only surprise him, it will also intrigue him, knowing you cared so much to go through the loving trouble. Write your love message in code, possibly using your private pet name for him. This gives you a great opportunity to dazzle him with special romantic surprise. You can express your feelings in just a few loving words. When the ad appears, circle it and leave it on the kitchen table when you leave for work. If you're not living together, call him at work on the day the ad appears and tell him there's a secret message for him on a certain page of the morning paper.

- **Loving Touches:** The need to be touched is embedded in us from the time we are first brought into the world. Research has proven that some small animals has actually died from the lack of touch. Touching is all about receiving and giving warmth to each other. Couples who have been together for years tend to forget how exciting it can be to feel the texture of silks and satins, shirts and trousers beneath their fingertips—the slow, erotic tease of touching a lover here and there through clothes, the arousing promise of reaching under a skirt or of touching a man through his pants. Once you get into touching each other, instead of just jumping into bed and going straight for the prize, new stimulating spots on each other's bodies will be discovered.

- Keep things sizzling in the bedroom with clear sexual signals.
- lace a surprise gift on his pillow.
- Walk up and give him a hug when he least expect it.
- Bring him to a state of arousal so high that it is inevitable & irresistible.
- Serve breakfast in bed after a night of passion.
- Shower together and soap each other up.
- Be forgiving and don't sweat the small stuff.
- Make his favorite meal once a week.
- Read poetry together on a lazy Sunday evening.
- A full body massage to relax before bed.
- Sing to him in your best romantic voice.
- Be playful in bed with erotic fantasies.
- Be carefree with your hands to explore every inch.
- Add variety to your routine by changing the place.
- Add anticipation with strawberries and cream at the bedside table.
- Use imagination with fresh cut flowers.
- Let your hair down and sweep it across his chest.
- Use different positions for different nights.
- Spice up your nights of passion with sensual oils.
- Use candles to heighten the mood.

- Use satin sheets on a warm summer night.

- Enhance the moment with chilled champagne.

- Express yourself with kisses.

- Keep it romantic with soft music.

- Be patient with flaring attitudes.

- Be tolerance of nagging habits.

- Candle-lit dinners just because.

- Feed each other foods that you can hold with your fingers.

- Use sincere compliments to warm the heart.

- Be supportive of his work.

- Give each other a foot massage.

- Be trusting of his word.

- Write him a love letter and mail it to his job's address.

- Raise the desire with satiny black or red lingerie.

- Mail a greeting card just because.

- Say I love you when he's feeling down.

- Watch romantic movies together

- Use different locations for making love: kitchen, den, etc.

- Initiate lovemaking

- Make love during the day

- Take interest in things your mate enjoys.

- Be positive and don't nag.

- Be accepting of the imperfections.

- Give him a warm shave.

- Moonlit walks just to hold hands and talk.

- Picnics on the balcony on warm summer evenings.
- Talk dirty on the phone.
- Love in the morning with the sun shining through.
- Find time for loving in the afternoon.
- Reserve time for loving in the evening before your energy fade.
- Dress sexy in black leather and lace for an audience of one.
- Red high-heels and nothing else.
- Give a single rose occasionally.
- Buy a gift just because.
- Cuddle every chance you can.
- Create occasions that the two of you can dress up.
- Spend extra time in bed together every chance you can.
- During intimate moments turn off the phone.
- Pillow Talk, whisper your undying love during lovemaking.
- Give each other back rubs.
- Leave a love note or card on the front seat of his car.
- Put a handful of his favorite candy in the glove compartment.
- Use dim lights to set the scene.
- Make dinner in a see-through teddy for an audience of one.
- Close the blinds, turn off the phone and create your own week-end hideaway.
- When he's upset, make him laugh by saying something like, "You look cute when you're mad."

Keep the flames in your relationship red hot and don't let the fire sizzle out! Work some of the 70 ways to love your lover into your relationship and watch the flames of love and passion grow.

Chapter 38

8 Great Ways to Stay Forever Young Looking and Fit

In any relationship how we look and take care of ourselves is key to making our partner happy. By keeping ourselves looking our best, we show that we care about ourselves and the one we're with. No matter how young or how beautiful or how fit we are at this time in our lives, we all realize it's just temporary—that age will catch up with us. And growing old may be apart of the beauty of living, but if we could continue to live and grow older without looking older that would be like a heaven sent!

But even though, we all look forward to one more birthday to celebrate and indulge in life. And as the years pile up, we don't mind growing old, we just don't want to look old or feel old. Because when we look into the mirror and see our reflection looking back at us, we would like for that reflection to reveal that we look young and healthy for whatever age we are. If we're 37, it's always nice to hear someone say, "You only look 27, or you look much younger than your age."

We all know that we grow older with each birthday, but now according to research, age is just a number, and doesn't always have to reflect how we look or feel. Recent research suggests that the body's gradual decline stems not from the passing of years but from the combined effects of inactivity and poor nutrition. So no matter what your present health status or your chronological age—regular exercise and improved eating habits will lower your biological age.

Aerobic Capacity:

The greater this aerobic capacity, the faster oxygen is pumped throughout our body—and the fitter we are. Regular aerobic exercise will raise your aerobic capacity no matter what your present age. The longer and harder your workouts, the greater the benefits.

Blood-Sugar Tolerance:

As we age, it brings about a gradual decline our body's ability to metabolize blood sugar, and by the time we reach age 70, 20 percent of men and 30 percent of women, we are at increased risk of diabetes. A low-fat, high-fiber diet, combined with regular exercise, will cut your risk of diabetes.

Body Fat Percentage:

In many cases, advancing age brings us not just muscle loss but fat gain; and even if our weight (as measured by a scale) changes just a little, the ratio of fat to lean in our bodies can rise markedly over the passing of birthdays. It's common knowledge that excessive amounts of fat can lead to chronic diseases and premature death, especially the fat around the waist, it's far more unhealthy than fat on the buttocks or thighs. To help yourself lose fat and gain muscle, combine a low-fat diet along with regular exercise.

Blood Pressure:

To keep your pressure in check, stay slim, and don't smoke, get regular exercise and limit your consumption of fat, salt and alcohol. If these steps fail, pressure lowering drugs may be necessary.

Bone Density:

As we age our skeletons slowly become weaker and more brittle. And while some mineral loss is inevitable, the severe and potentially deadly condition known as osteoporosis is not. Consuming at least 800 milligrams of calcium a day will retard the loss of bone, but just that alone rarely does the trick. Also needed is weight-bearing exercise, such as walking, running or cycling.

Muscle Mass:

As we move from adolescence into our golden years, we lose almost seven pounds of lean body mass each decade—a rate that accelerates after age 45. And reduced muscle mass leads not only to reduced strength, but also to an increased risk of heart disease and diabetes, reduced aerobic capacity and a slower metabolism (which promotes fat gain). You can help keep your muscle mass by staying active. You can take walks to short distances instead of driving, and you can get in a habit of using the stairs instead of the elevator. And maybe try doing some of your own indoor and outdoor chores instead or letting younger friends or relatives do them for you.

Strength:

Between the ages of 20 and 70, we lose about 30 percent of this muscle cells—including a large proportion of "fast-twitch" cells needed for sprinting and other high-exertion exercise. And if left unchecked, this loss of muscle leads eventually to sarcopenia, the severe, debilitating weakness that makes independent living impossible, and while there is no way we cannot prevent loss of our muscle cells, starting a weight-lifting regimen can compensate by boosting the size and strength of the cells that remain. (Always check with your doctor before starting a new exercise routine).

Metabolic Rate:

Because more energy is needed to maintain muscle than fat, the less muscle tissue in your body, the slower your metabolism—and the fewer calories you must consume to maintain ideal body weight. Beginning at 20, the average person's metabolic rate drops about two percent per decade. Example: average 70 year old needs 500 fewer calories a day than the average 25 year old. To assist in fighting fat, eat fewer calories and get enough exercise to maintain your muscle mass.

Follow these eight ways to stay forever young looking and fit and look and feel your best all your life!

Chapter 39

10 Secrets to Sexual Fitness

Most of us are aware that we need to exercise for fitness and health, but many of us may not know that we need the same workouts for sexual fitness. And whether you workout from time to time or have a regular routine already in place, according to Dr. Hank Wuh, in his book, *Sexual Fitness, 7 Essential Elements To Optimizing Your Sensuality, Satisfaction and Well-Being,* you have even more of an incentive: "Exercise will improve your sex life," says Dr. Wuh. And if you're wondering how? He explains that "Exercise builds endurance, flexibility and muscle strength."

Just as important, Dr. Wuh explains that exercise has an impact on your sex life by enhancing your self-esteem and increasing your physical stamina. Exercise also boosts production of key sex hormones. Several studies have shown that testosterone levels rise just after short periods of intense exercise. Over time, your body will change in ways that facilitate better sex.

Listed below are 10 of the secrets that Dr. Wuh recommends to get you to sexual fitness:

- **Enjoyable Activities:** Pick Activities that you enjoy. Don't force yourself to run if you hate running, because you won't keep it up. You can walk, swim, bicycle, do aerobics or practice yoga. You can learn to box, golf, ballroom dance or bowl. The specific activities you choose matter far less than the fact that you like them.

- **Seek Convenience:** Make sure exercising is convenient. The activities you select should be easy for you to do. Don't choose swimming as your form of exercise if it takes an hour-long special trip to get to the pool. Try to work out near either your home or work. Make sure that you have options for physical activities whether it's raining, snowing or a bright sunny day.

- **Reject Boredom:** Don't let yourself get bored. Experiment with new activities. For example, if you like ice skating, try in-line skating. Also, rather than taking the same class or doing the same workout every day of the week, rotate your schedule. Swim one day, then do aerobics the next. Do a long-distance run for one workout, and then do sprints for the next. By keeping yourself entertained, you are more likely to stay motivated.

- **Exercise Buddies:** Work out with a buddy. Exercise buddies will help motivate you and prevent you from coming up with excuses for not working out. You can motivate your buddy, too. You're a lot less likely to skip a walk around the park or trip to the gym if you know that your friend is counting on you, and vice versa. Some people enjoy working out with their partners.

  Exercising together gives couples time to enjoy each other in the midst of their busy lives—and you may even end up in the bedroom for a different kind of workout!

- **Take Classes:** Take classes or join an activity group. A trained instructor will be able to help address your specific needs, give you advice on how to stay fit, and keep you motivated. Also, being part of a group will ensure that you have regularly scheduled activities to attend, so you'll be less likely to skip your workouts. Aside from classes at a gym, many communities have walking groups, running clubs, soccer or basketball teams.

- **Stretch:** Make time to stretch. Start your workouts with a warm-up. Get your muscles heated with about five minutes of physical activity, then stretch. Stretch again for at least five minutes at the end of your workout. Stretching will reduce your risk of injury, prevent you from getting sore and make you more flexible.

- **Begin Today:** Begin today—no excuses. Don't tell yourself, "I'll start next week because I have a big project due Friday," or "I just need to get over this little cold." As soon as you check with your physician to make sure that it's okay, get started with your new exercise routine. Put on a pair of tennis shoes and take a walk around the house. Join a gym. Walk up a flight of stairs. You may only do 10 minutes of physical activity, but you will have taken the first critical steps—both physically and mentally. Start today!

- **Start Slowly:** Don't push yourself too hard, especially at first. You've got to give your body time to get used to the idea of exercise and you certainly don't want to begin by injuring yourself. So do what you can, but don't overdo it. You'll know when you're ready for more. Also, be sure to allow yourself a day of rest after a strenuous workout.

- **Your Body:** Listen to your body. If you have a sore knee, don't keep pushing yourself to walk harder and faster. Pay attention to your aches and pains. You do not want a mild irritation to become a serious injury, which could potentially slow you down for months. So when your body says "Stop," do it. Then make an appointment to see your physician and figure out how you can fix the problem before it gets worse.

- **Set Goals:** Make weekly goals for yourself—think about what you will achieve and write it down. A goal can be as simple as "I'm going to go to the gym four times this week." Once you get more advanced, you can set yourself more complex goals, such as "I'm going to take five minutes off my running time." If you really want to make sure that you'll stick to your goals, share them with another person. You'll be less likely to cheat if you do.

Chapter 40

10 Tips to Maintaining a Lasting Relationship

One major key to a everlasting bond is to be able to share your feelings with each other. We need to have a person in our life with whom we can openly and safely share our feelings. It is very powerful to be able to share your every feeling and trust that they will still love you and not hurt you with criticism, judgment, or rejection. When you can share who you are and how you feel, then you can fully receive love. If you have this love, it is easier to release negative emotional symptoms like resentment, anger, and fear.

The bottom line is crystal clear, in order for two people to build and maintain a lasting relationship, it takes continuous work and effort, without which, you can look around and discover your relationship has gone flat, headed toward a break up. Follow the ten tips to help maintain a lasting relationship!

Expressing Love:

Recognize that one method of expression isn't enough! Love can be and should be expressed in many ways. But most of us settle into one mode that's comfortable for us. And while it's familiar to you, it becomes boring for your partner. And he also explains that some of you are verbal, and you share your feelings a lot. That's great. But you've got to back it up with some modes of expression that communicate caring on other levels, too. Express your love through sharing in each other's hobbies.

Romancing:

Find time to include as much romance in your relationship as possible, like adding a vase of fresh flowers on the dinner table, playing soft romantic music at bedtime. On some occasions, have candlelight dinners and breakfast in bed, and maybe every once in a while a champagne picnic in the backyard

Communicating:

It's vital in any relationship to keep the lines of communication open, letting each other know how you feel and what you're thinking. Having heart-to-hearts helps couples stay close. If something your partner does bother you, talk to him and encourage him to do the same. Set aside some time to be alone together to have more intimate conversations. Just bear in mind that good communication in a relationship is similar to a solid foundation in a house. If a house is built with a strong foundation, it will be able to withstand the stress caused by such natural disasters as hurricanes or tornadoes. Even if the rest of the house is damaged or destroyed, if the foundation is solid the house can be rebuilt.

Be Forgiving:

If he did something that really disappointed/hurt you, but he seems sincerely sorry about it, just accept his apology. To fully open our hearts to each other and enjoy a lifetime of love, the most important thing of all is forgiveness. The more you love someone, the more you suffer when you don't forgive them. The greatest pain we can ever feel is the pain of not loving someone we love. Real forgiveness acknowledges that a real mistake has been made and then affirms that the person who made it still deserves to be loved and respected.

Being Best Friends:

Starting out as friends is the key to a long lasting relationship. Friendship along with sex is the cement. Lovers rarely stay lovers without friendship. Friendship is praising strengths instead of criticizing weaknesses. Friendship cushions you against the inevitable fall off those first ecstatic high peaks of early romance. If there is a strong bond of friendship between you, you can accept the lows along with the highs. Your friendship will keep you connected. Just like the saying, a man's best friend is his dog. It's because a dog gives his owner unconditional love and doesn't put down or call his owner stupid—regardless to what his owner says or does. The same kind of unconditional love and kindness that a man gets from his dog is the kind of kindness and consideration he wants from his woman. He wants a friend to lift him up and make him feel good about himself. Friendship is being there when you are needed, helping to fight your partner's battles, and soothing your partner's wounds. In another sense, friendship is the nonsexual side of intimacy—sharing your experiences, plans, hopes, and frustrations. Romance attracts, friendship holds.

Romance is the perfume and spice of intimacy; friendship is the cement. Lovers rarely stay lovers without friendship. Friendship is praising strengths instead of criticizing weaknesses. Friendship is being there when you are needed, helping to fight your partner's battles, and soothing your partner's wounds. She explains that in another sense, friendship is the nonsexual side of intimacy—sharing your experiences, plans, hopes, and frustrations. Friendship cushions you against the inevitable fall off those first ecstatic high peaks of early romance. If there is a strong bond of friendship between you, you can accept the lows along with the highs.

Showing Trust:

Try for honesty with your mate at all time. Lay your cards on the table. Tell him about your weaknesses as well as your strong points. Let him know your likes and dislikes. Let him see the whole you, the real you. Be honest and on the level at the beginning of your relationship, there should be no major surprises. Some surprises can lead to mistrust. Mistrust can lead to the downfall of your relationship.

Entering into a relationship is like walking with a blindfold on, it all boils down to trust. And in a lasting, meaningful relationship—trusting each other should come as easy as breathing. If it doesn't, it's like a constant fight against itself. In a case where there's no trust, what's the point of even trying to make it work. But often times in a relationship, many of us feel the hell with trusting him, because it just isn't in the cards it seems. But think again! Focus on your bottom line, which is to be able to maintain a lasting relationship. Doing so, trust has to be a part of the package. According to *Webster's New World Dictionary*, the definition of trust is "A firm belief in another's honesty, reliability." This means, if he goes out with the guys for the evening, you won't ask too many questions or get upset. And if he happens to get home late from work sometimes you won't get upset. Because, frankly, if you don't trust him, he will know it. Once he senses mistrust, automatically his heart locks, keeping it clear of lasting love. When a woman's attitude is open and receptive toward a man he feels trusted. To trust a man is to believe that he is doing his best and that he wants the best for his partner. The secret to growing in trust is not to expect your man to be perfect. Try and understand how men are different, and enable yourself to trust that he loves you even when he doesn't instinctively do the things you would do to demonstrate caring.

Chapter 41

9 Great Ways to Feel Sexy About Yourself

Some days it seems like the work day is never going to end, when it does, you get home to more chaos: needy kids and a demanding mate; and the clock continues to tick. Pretty soon it's time to start the same day all over again. And with your plate overflowing, you could easily say, "I don't have time to think of myself or feeling sexy." But never consider such a thought!

Even with demands coming from all directions, the kids, your man, your boss and even the neighbors, always take time for yourself and be your sexiest. As a woman, it's your birth-right!

If you ask one hundred men, "What is sexy?" ninety-nine of them will probably say something like "self-confidence" or "self-assurance." They really don't care that much if a woman is beautiful or has a god-dess-like form. What they really think is sexy is the woman who is confident and feels good about herself and her body. But even so, so many females just don't feel attractive or comfortable with their bodies. Many prefer to always keep the lights dimmed or turned off altogether when they are intimate with their partner, thinking in the back of their minds, my hips are too large, my thighs are too fat, trying not to show much of themselves. And this boils down to, there's a lot of women out there who don't think they're sexy. And even more, thinking they don't have the time or energy to even think of being sexy. But being confident about yourself is an energizing force within itself.

Here are some of the words men use most often when they try to explain what "sexy" means to them: Self-confidence, fit, femininity, intelligence, attractive, friendliness, healthy, well-groomed and self-assurance.

Regardless of what the media and large billboards say, a woman does not have to be a beauty queen or have a flawless figure to be considered truly sexy in the eyes of a man. And it goes without saying, that the majority of the insecurities and fears that burden females are amplified from what is shown on TV and at the movies, and of course, paging through one of your favorite fashion magazines, which states that people with stunning faces and perfect bodies are the ones who are viewed as truly sexy.

If you are wondering by now, what does it take to feel sexy? According to author, Alexandra Penney, simply this: "The more you are comfortable and at ease with yourself and your body, the more sexy and attractive you will feel, and you must feel sexy in order to be sexy."

9 Ways To Feel More Sexy About Yourself:

Think Positively About Your Appearance:
Very few people have super bodies or flawless faces, and it's important to keep this thought in mind. If you don't, you're likely to fall into some very common traps that you can set for yourself about how you look: the "either I look terrific or I look terrible" trap, the "he's going to notice my blemishes" trap, and the "constant comparison" trap. There will always be a body or a face better than yours, so if you see yourself in these negative terms, you're inevitably going to assume that there's something not right about you, and you'll constantly feel inadequate and unattractive.

Suppose, now you know the traps, you still aren't please with yourself. The best, quickest, and most efficient course of action is to start a serious diet and/or exercise program.

Diet/Exercise:
The minute you begin your diet/or exercise program, regardless to whether you workout in front of your bedroom mirror every morning or start eating one piece of toast instead of two, the process of feeling more self-assured and more sexy has begun.

Your Makeup:
Wear your make up regularly and make sure it's becoming and applied neatly. And if you're not in the habit of wearing makeup, start out with a little bit of lipstick or lip gross. It will make you look and feel more sexy!

Your Hair:
To feel your sexiest, your hair has to be in order. If your hair isn't in order, no matter how well you are dressed or how well your makeup is applied, you still won't feel sexy or look becoming. (A visit to a hairdresser makes a woman feel pampered and sexy) If you style your own hair, keep it styled and looking clean and healthy every single day. But if you go to the salon, of course, you won't be going there every day. Because hairdressers can get kind of costly. Yet, to feel your sexiest, you should keep an appointment with your hairdresser at least once every week, or try not to wait any longer than every two weeks.

Hands/Nails/Feet:
Keep your hands and nails and feet looking smooth and sexy and well-groomed with the polish of your choice. Besides from feeling sexy with sexy hands and feet, taking the time to care for your hands, nails and feet are quite important to your man. "Over and over again, men from every social and economic background say that they check out details such as makeup, hair, nails, and skin. They don't need to be with a stunning woman, but they definitely do prefer women who take time to make themselves look their best.

Pampering & Caring For Yourself:

Pampering yourself is one sure way to feel sexy. Set aside one evening a week for yourself. You may stay home and take a long, warm bath. Play beautiful music, light candles, and either read a wonderful book or turn down the lights and fantasize. Take the time to do what you would most enjoy doing.

Lavish In Your Femininity:

Never miss an opportunity to let a man carry a box for you or open the door; it doesn't mean you need him to open the door or carry a box for you, but it will make you feel sexy every time he does. Plus he'll feel good too.

Massages:

Make it a regular routine to pamper yourself. Ask your Partner to give you a massage once in a while. Getting a massage or some kind of nurturing body work every week is very valuable in being sexy.

Nonsexual Touches:

Being touched and caressed by your man in a Soothing non-sexual way is a very important method of feeling sexy and relaxing from the demands of the workday to bring you back to a pleasant awareness of your body.

Pampering and caring for yourself is not self-indulgence. It's simply, taking the time to think of yourself the way you take the time to think of others.

Pampering yourself is one sure way to feel your sexiest. Do it! You can have it all. The demands of a full-time career! The love of your life! kids! And yet never lose sight of your own femininity by always making sure you feel your sexiest.

Chapter 42

14 Ways to Stop Trying to Change Him

When we fall in love, our world seem brighter and we want to keep it that way. Right away we start a campaign on ways to try to improve our relationship, but in our effort to make our affair stronger and everlasting, we dump our mate right over into the improvement basket along with everything else. And even though, we may not mean any harm by the little things we want him to change, like picking up his socks or emptying his cigar ashes, he will see them as "harm" being rejected. According to Dr. John Gray, in his book, *Men Are From Mars, Women Are From Venus,* "In a myriad of ways she tries to change him or improve him. She thinks her attempts to change him are loving, but he feels controlled, manipulated, rejected, and unloved. He will stubbornly reject her because he feels she is rejecting him."

If we had the sun too much we would want the rain, and if we had the rain too much we would want the sun. Our differences are what makes us so attracted to each other. But, on the other hand, because no one is exactly like us, many times in our relationships we want to change or make our mate over. But instead of trying to change and make him over, we need to appreciate and accept him for who he is and not allow a few little habits to get under our skin, because just imagine what your relationship would be like if your partner agreed with everything you said or did. Being with someone like that would be no different than talking to a rag doll sitting on a shelf. A complete bore!

Any attempt to change him takes away the loving trust, acceptance, appreciation, admiration, approval, and encouragement that are his primary needs.

The root of this situation is one we should really take to heart, because whether we mean any harm or not in our efforts to try and change him, we're stripping him of his complete self. So it's wise to never try to change him or improve him.

It's as simple as men thinking they know what's going on in our heads when we're upset, we think we know what's best for our mate and why they behave the way they do. Just as men mistakenly want to "fix" women, women mistakenly try to "improve" men. Men see things differently from us and their motto is "don't fix it, if it isn't broken." When a woman attempts to change a man, he receives the message that she thinks he is broken. This hurts a man and makes him very defensive. He doesn't feel loved and accepted.

A man is no different from us in wanting to be accepted and appreciated regardless of his imperfections. But when it comes to the man we love it's hard to accept their little faults, especially when we feel we know exactly how he could become better. It does, however, become easier when we understand that the best way to help him grow is to let go of trying to change him in any way.

- Remember: don't ask him to many questions when he is upset or he will feel you are trying to change him.

- Ignore that he is upset unless he wants to talk to you about it. Show some initial concern, but not too much, as an invitation to talk.

- Remember: give up trying to improve him in any way. He needs your love, not rejection, to grow.

189

- Trust him to grow on his own. Honestly share feelings but without the demand that he change.

- Remember: when you offer unsolicited advice he may feel mistrusted, controlled, or rejected.

- Practice patience and trust that he will learn on his own what he needs to learn. Wait until he asks for your advice.

- Remember: when a man becomes stubborn and resists change he is not feeling loved; he is afraid to admit his mistakes for fear of not being loved.

- Practice showing him that he doesn't have to be perfect to deserve your love. Practice forgiving.

- Remember: if you make sacrifices hoping he will do the same for you then he will feel pressured to change.

- Practice doing things for yourself and not depending on him to make you happy.

- Remember: you can share negative feelings without trying to change him. When he feels accepted it is easier for him to listen.

- When sharing feelings, let him know that you are not trying to tell him what to do but that you want him to take your feelings into consideration.

- Remember: if you give him directions and make decisions for him he will feel corrected and controlled.

- Relax and surrender. Practice accepting imperfection. Make his feelings more important than perfection and don't lecture or correct him.

When two people enter into a relationship, their love can be as strong as steel, but it's not the strength of their love that will carry them all the way, it will be their ability to trust, accept, appreciate and admire their partner for who they are. And the biggest obstacle of all is learning to deal with each other's little habits and not try to change each other. Once you can get past that, the rest is smooth sailing!

Chapter 43

6 Ways to Hold Onto Love

Always and forever you can hold on to the love you have won! How do you do this? You do it with your charm! Your amazing grace and patience That's right, he can be yours forever and fall head over-heels in love with you and never stop falling. All it takes is to "treat the man you are really, really crazy about like the man you're not that interested in—don't call, be busy sometimes! Think about how you would behave if you weren't interested in a guy, and just treat your beloved the way you would treat a man that you weren't that crazy over. And no need to worry that your dream boat will walk away from you while you're playing semi-hard to get. Case and point: The men you don't like keep calling after you've turned them down, don't they?

Think for a second, have you ever wondered why some guy from your past or the guy next door is still in love with you, why he still calls and talks to your mother about you? And why he still wants to take you out, even when you keep ignoring him? He has never gotten over you. You were the challenge of his life. The one he was never able to conquer.

Now think of your present affair. You love and adore your boyfriend, but sometimes, you feel as if you're pushing him away, but you're wondering how could that be? You're treating him like a king. You buy him things! You send him cards! You call him five or six times a day! You give him all your time and attention! But the more you do, the more he just seems to take you for granted. It could be other reasons, but likely, he sees you as no challenge. Men can easily bore when they can have their cake and eat it too. Make sure he's yours always and forever by keeping him in love with you. How? By being totally wild for him, but not letting it shine through so much by your over anxious actions. Don't let him see you boil over—just let him see you sizzle. Give him the challenge that most men want. The challenge of you being a complete woman; someone who loves him, but also have your own life and interest.

Men are born to respond to challenge. Take away challenge and their interest wanes. If men love challenge, we become challenging! But don't ask a man if he loves challenge. He may think or even say he doesn't. He may not even realize how he reacts. Pay attention to what he does, not what he says.

Be Easy To Love:
Be friendly and easy to love and that will surely keep him smiling. Everybody loves to be around a happy, fun loving person. Men especially love the company of cheerful females. Try to be in a good mood. A huffy attitude tends to scare men away. When the screaming and yelling starts, he's out the door. Men can be very intimidated by what we say and how we say it. Sometimes we may not mean any harm, and we may not mean to come off so fussy like. But we do cause harm when we nag and fly off the handle about too many little things.

Don't Try Changing Him:
You want to be with him always and forever. He's your dream man, but there are a few things about him that you wish were different. What do you do? Nothing! Don't try to change him because men are no different from us when it comes to this subject. We can't change them anymore than they can change us. You either have to accept him completely as he is, with his flaws and all or find someone else. If you try to attempt to change him in any way, he will loathe the thought. It

could take something away from the special feeling he has for you. The sure-fire rules to keep him in love go straight out of the window.

Don't Go Overboard On Gifts:
Men love gifts as much as we do, but like to be the one giving the most of them. The bottom line is not to shower or lavish him with too many gifts and things and make him feel you're taking the lead. For special occasions like his birthday, Christmas and Valentine Day is okay. But otherwise, don't spend too much time shopping for him. When you start buying things for a man, they think you are hen-pecked, and when they think that, their interest start to fade. The challenge is over.

Don't Crowd Him:
When the two of you go out to a party or dancing, don't smother him by holding on to his arm. Let him mingle with his friends and associates if he wants to. If you get upset and try to keep him right by your side, he may oblige you just to keep you happy. But he won't be happy and will probably feel trapped. He may not be too interested in taking you to the next party or dance. He may start going out without you altogether, and if you ask him to take you out dancing or to a party, don't be surprise if he says, "At the last party you were no fun."

Keep Up Your Looks:
A woman's looks are extremely important to a man. Whether he admits it or not. They are first attracted by the physical. The more physically attractive a woman is to a man, the less he needs to think or discern. He automatically behaves as if she is the most special woman in the world. To keep him by our side always and forever, we'll have to keep up our appearance. Some guys think of their women as a special prize. In his eyes (the better she looks. The better he'll look). Show him that you care about yourself and how you look. Keep your hair looking neat, your makeup applied neatly, your nails manicured, and always dress your sexy best around him.

Don't Phone Too Much:

Whenever you take a trip or go out with the boys or even at work, don't keep the phone lines too busy. By all means, call him when you please, just don't call him six or seven times a day. You're doing it because you adore him and can't stop thinking about him, but if you continue to do it, he'll find it annoying and will start making excuses why he can't talk. Worse yet, he'll think you don't have a life. Not just men, nobody likes to be bothered that much. Most people can think of at less one person who they hate talking to on the phone, because that person calls too much. Think about when an ex-boyfriend or some other guy you used to know, how their constant calls turned you off. Someone who continually calls someone too often is thought of as a pest. People like to stay clear of a pest. Calling him too often is a way to make him lose interest.

Chapter 44

Are You Living an Illusion of Love?

Picture this! Your life being performed on a stage in front of you. You're in a relationship sharing your life, your hopes, your dreams and your desires, and even your bed. The picture is painted to your liking. Then, one day you wake up and find that the artist has made changes to the portrait! The sweet illusion has vanished and suddenly you don't want to be where you are! If you can picture that, now answer this? Have you looked deep down inside of you to figure out how you really feel about the man in your life, and why you are really with him in the first place? If it's not because you love and adore him to pieces, then ask yourself? Are you in love with the man in your life, or could it be possible that you are just living an illusion? Now, maybe you are asking yourself, I'm not sure. How can I know? And you might even think, I don't even care to know if I am living an illusion. Why should I care? Well, first thing first. In order for us to be able to learn how to create positive loving relationships in our lives, to make sure we don't fall into that illusion trap, it is important to understand that what often seems like love may actually be an illusion of love. And how do you tell true love from an illusion of love? You can ask yourself a few questions, like, "would I be happy with the man in my life if we lived in the middle of the desert, on top of an isolation mountain or in the middle of a forest in a tree house?" And if your answer is yes, than your love for him is not an illusion.

Illusions of love are created by our ego, which is interested only in getting its own needs met. And the very foundation for illusions of love is not solid, which means, being wrapped up in this kind of an affair will always end in heartbreak for one of the parties.

The illusions of love take many different forms. For example, when both people's selfish needs are met in a relationship, their ego feels as if it's on top of the world. Most of us, at some point or another have experienced this as the "honeymoon period" of a relationship, an illusion that is the basis for "romantic love." This illusion lasts only as long as both people's needs are being met, and when either feels that his or her needs are not met, one or both parties become frustrated, and this frustration can quickly turn into anger.

Shirley, 51, Nurses Aide:

Lived an illusion of love for over twenty-five years with her husband, who was a 52-year-old retired military officer, in the hope that the man she was married to would change into the Prince charming that he wasn't. "For years I lived an illusion of love. All I wanted was him, since I couldn't have him, I left the rest behind. I was married for over twenty-five years in a marriage to a man I slaved for. I did everything for him under the sun and I kept waiting for the day to come that he would return my love and look around and see what a treasure he had in me. But the weeks and months passed and soon I had given up most of my life to just hope. I gave him two daughters and watched them grow, get through high school and begin college. I watched him ignore his own grandson because he couldn't stand his own daughter who gave birth to him.

I wake up one morning and realized that I didn't have much time left for happiness. At 47, I was pushing fifty fast. I asked him straight out for his love and affection and he said, "You have a big house and all these things that I have worked hard to give you, why do you want more. I don't have any love or affection to give you." When he said that, he said it all. I had to make a choice to either stay with a man who would stay with me just because he had a maid, a cook, and a slave or I could leave and give up everything I had worked dearly for. My nearly thirty-year marriage, my job, my new home, all my nice furnishings, my neighbors and friends and coworkers. I could keep it all and continue to starve for love and affection in a loveless marriage or I could give up all of that and him and find real love and happiness. I chose the latter. I headed to work one day and in the process, turned my car around and drove none stop to my mother's home over twelve hours away. I never looked back. I have a new life now. I'm starting over with a new job in a new living quarters. Where I am and what I have is a far cry from what I gave up. But I have a peace of mind and a chance for love and affection. And if I never find the love and affection that I crave. At least, I'm not giving up my life with a man who could only take and never give.

Cathy, 31, Banker:

Cathy and her boyfriend, Junior, a 41-year-old brain surgeon, had dated for several months, Junior loved Cathy, but she wasn't truly in love with him. "I just dated Junior because of his position. I was excited to be asked out by a brain surgeon. It's real clear to me now, since I'm no longer with him. I wasn't really in love with Junior but told myself I was. I know now it was just an illusion of love. Being attracted to who he was, because after the malpractice suit and he lost his license, he was just another man in my eyes. I lost interest and stopped going out with him."

After Junior position and status was ripped from him and he was forced to seek a position other than the brain surgeon he was, just a regular guy without the status of being an upstanding doctor, Cathy's illusion faded. What had looked like love just a while ago has now become a love/hate relationship. Whether we use words or not, we send to each other a massage that "I will love you only so long as you give me what I want." This is the basis of the illusion we call "conditional love."

Our ego knows about fear, but it can't understand the deepest part of us, which is love, and since our ego can't understand love, that sits it apart from love, not being able to experience it either. The ego's form of love is always conditional and is always an illusion. It's favorite theme is: "I will love you and stay with you if..." The big emphasis, of course, is on the "if."

Emma, 39, Nurse's Assistant:

Emma was married to Lawrence, a 44-year-old army officer for 18 years who only had an illusion of love for her. "It was always about what he wanted, and what made him happy. If I worked all week and gave him all of my paycheck to go into the saving account along with his, he was happy and would show be affection. But if I used some of the money I worked for to buy myself personal items, he would with-draw his love and wouldn't touch me in bed. After the kids moved out on their own, I left too."

The ego is ambivalent about love and doesn't see sex as a way of shar-ing feelings of love, tenderness, caring, and gentleness toward another person. Rather, it sees sex as a trade or bargain and an oppor-tunity for controlling and manipulating another person to serve its own selfish needs. It may use sex as a form of anger by communicat-ing "I am angry at you, so I'll punish you by not having sex with you." The ego may also use sex as a token to trade for financial security; the silent message being "I don't love you, but having sex with you is a way of holding on to you and the security that your money offers me." This was the case with Charlene and Travis.

Charlene 27, Waitress:

"I was a 17-year-old high school dropout with no job, living at home receiving a welfare check for my two toddlers when I met Travis, who was 25 at the time," says Charlene. "He had a good job and his own house that he owned. My focus was to get out of my parents house and take care of my two boys. I moved in with Travis and became his live in girlfriend for the security and financial benefits," she explains. "A year and a half later, after I got my GED and was able to get a decent job and take care of my own kids, my illusion faded for him. Suddenly, I didn't want to be with him because I didn't need his help any more. We broke up and I moved out of his house into my own apartment."

The ego is very good at creating these illusions of love, and it is capable of putting sex and love in separate compartments; completely dissociated from one another.

That's why so many sexual relationships can give the illusion of love when they may have nothing to do with love. They may be focused not on giving love to another person but only on getting one's own bodily needs satisfied. This is why in many sexual relationships the sex becomes boring. When we dissociate sex from love, sexual relationships became so mechanical that it is like two robots trying to communicate without feelings.

When it comes to love, our ego believes that we always suffer from great scarcity. Relationships simply don't work when they are based on this illusion. The ego's image is that we have a "gas tank" for love, and the gauge is always hovering around empty, causing us to be constantly looking for a refill, controlling and manipulating other people in order to get its own needs met, having absolutely no interest in, nor capacity for, unconditional Love; where there is total acceptance, no assumptions, expectations, or demands, and where there is no desire to "get something" from the other person.

Unconditional love does not mean putting up with hurtful behavior, it means a willingness to see past someone's little habits and flaws and to choose to see the essence of love that is the spiritual being of that person in your life.

This concept is often misunderstood, for instances, a woman may be married to an alcoholic who physically and emotionally abuses her, and yet she stays in that situation, where she continues to get punished. The wife may think she is staying because of love, but that is an illusion of love. Often that person stays in an abusive situation out of fear and guilt, where she unconsciously believes that she somehow deserves the beatings she receives.

A person with healthy self-esteem who also loves unconditionally does not stay in an abusive situation. The true essence of love is experienced not with illusions of love based on the drive to "get," nor on illusions of love based on punishment of any kind. Unconditional love refers to the "content" of our love rather than the "form." It means accepting the love of our spiritual self and choosing to look beyond the body and personality-self of the other person to see the spiritual essence within him or her.

Chapter 45

Your Love Life Deserves a Sensual Holiday

In the beginning of your marriage when everything is fresh and your pleasures together are like being in paradise, you lose yourself in the good times. Your mind doesn't give a hint to any other thoughts except how wonderful things are between you and your mate. You don't think about the time that it could be anything else, but maybe we should think ahead, having a plan in mind, making sure the good times remain, keeping our affair fresh. No pleasure is forever; the moment disappears and the pleasures are gone. You can go back, but you can't go back very often. Time and people change. The same thing wears pleasure down. The same time, the same place, the same way, and the same face.

We need to use preventive measures to keep our pleasures long lasting. When we burn ourselves out at work we take a vacation, giving ourselves time to relax and recharge—coming back to our jobs feeling fresh and energized. Just think about it, if it can work wonders for our professional lives, it can work the same magic in our private lives. Why not give our relationship a sensual holiday, we take vacations and special days for everything else, we need the same kind of fresh start and relaxation for our relationships—to keep things exciting.

With our busy careers, our kids, our in-laws, and other responsibilities pulling from all directions, it's no wonder "Mr. Boredom" can walk right through our bedroom door. When "Mr. Boredom" settles in your bedroom, he sometimes becomes an invisible fixture, making it almost impossible to notice him sitting there, until, of course, he squeezing one of you out! That happens when you get so deep into a repetitive rut that your affair comes tumbling down around you.

Your eyes are open, but just be aware, making sure your love affair doesn't fall prey to old "Mr. Boredom." Give your relationship a sensual holiday and keep things fresh and vital. A sensual holiday is no more than an hour, a day, or a week when you leave your old habits and routines behind. A way of bringing the warmth of springtime to cold winter days, a way of bringing true romance and sizzling passion back into your relationship, to add great adventure and heighten your pleasures; to give yourself a chance to be playful and loving. A time to try new things, maybe something you have always wanted to try. A time to improve your sexual communication and put your cares and worries aside to just celebrate each other. A time when the two of you have decided to stop the world and get off—to have a look in another direction.

When planning your sensual holiday, you might even plan to spend a whole day in bed. The sky is the limit. You and your mate get to pick and choose where you spend or how you spend your sensual holiday. But make sure wherever you go or whatever you do, involve and indulge all your senses, so that, for at least, on that day, that evening or that weekend, you can become creatures of pleasure and romance. Listed below are a few sensual suggestions toward giving your relationship a sensual holiday. Remember you and your man deserve it!

Show Your Good Mood:
Start your sensual holiday with a good mood. Put an instant smile on your face and forget the fact that you were angry with him yesterday for forgetting to pick up your things from the dry-cleaners or that you were upset this morning that he didn't pick up his shoes. Start

your sensual holiday with those thoughts in the recycle bin. Because, as much as we want to cherish our love and keep our relationship on solid ground, sometimes we get stuck in a rut of feeling so comfortable with our mate that we forget we have to keep being thoughtful and considerate to keep that person in love with us. As strong as love is, it's just as fragile. That's why a person can be in love today and pack their bags and move out tomorrow. The point is, anyone can get an attitude, but if we continue to nag and fuss about everything under the sun all the time, he will eventually grow cold toward the relationship and leave. Show him your smile/good mood—so he can feel your love. He chiefly feels loved when you lets him know again and again that he is doing a good job of fulfilling you. A man is happiest when a woman is fulfilled.

A Picnic Indoors:
You can start your sensual holiday by preparing a romantic dinner and serving it on your finest China right on the middle of the living room floor. Sitting in front of the fireplace enjoying your meal or eating by candlelight is very romantic. You may want to consider serving finger foods, like grapes, cherries, and small pieces of melon and maybe some cut vegetables with your favorite dip. Nothing heavy or very filling, you'll need room for your icy cold sparkling champagne and dessert: chocolate mouse, strawberry Jell-O or French vanilla ice-cream. You name it, it's yours! If you're on a diet, today you get to cheat. You're on your sensual holiday and the only thing that matters is yours & his relaxation and sensual time!

An Evening Out:
Allow no excuse to stop your evening out with your mate. You may look at your desk and all the work you have piled high, and think to yourself, "I got to call him and cancel. I got to mark this evening off the calendar. There's no way I can squeeze in the time to go to the movies with him." You may think, "How can I get a baby-sitter at this short notice? But you can find a baby-sitter just like you know your work will be waiting for you the next day. So let nothing stop you from setting aside an evening out for you and your mate. Try for once

a week, and if you can manage twice a week that's even better. Because giving the two of you time out on the town, enjoying and discovering new places and things to do together. Because, all too often after a couple has been married for awhile or has dated for awhile—spending an evening out together get marked off of the list for one reason or another. One or the other decides there's no fun in eating out, going to the movies, going dancing or doing anything outside of their four walls. They have each other and they feel they don't need anything else. But that's the wrong frame of mind. And that frame of mind has watched many couples march into divorce court and say good-bye to what they thought was a solid union. Couples need the excitement and the adventure of doing things together. Couples who lean toward no fun time also lean toward building a split in their love life. These outings will serve as much needed glue in keeping the romance in your affair. The outings will also add adventure and bring some dazzle into your love life together.

A Lover's Massage:
Take turns giving each other massages with warm sweet smelling oils and lotions. You can start with gentle touches and communicate as you touch; by communicating as you caress an arm or rub a shoulder, your partner can tell you when to apply more pressure and when to touch lightly, telling you what's good and what's not so good. Rubbing the forehead, neck, shoulders, legs, or barefoot are great ways to relieve tension and be affectionate.

Remember that your sensual holiday is to teach each other to focus on sensuality; and it's about the two of you learning to put less emphasis on performance. Which means, you can kiss, touch, and caress your mate solely for your own pleasure.

Pleasures are like rainbows that are radiant, but can fade with the wind. Give your relationship a sensual holiday and keep your pleasures about now and not about then!

Chapter 46

The World of Married Life

There's nothing quite like meeting that special person and falling in love and finally walking down the aisle together. Life and everything around you seems perfect when you finally end up with that one special someone. Most of us get married for love and expect our union to last a lifetime, and we should expect that, after all, would we spend most of our savings for a beautiful wedding if we thought the marriage would only last for a short time? Of course not, we wouldn't bother at all. We marry because we want our marriage to last. But it's sad to say that more and more marriages are ending in divorce. And when you think about it, getting a divorce is similar to buying a new car, the old car isn't working right, so you'll trade it in for a new one. But marriage is a lot more precious than a vehicle or any piece of property. So, in order to get the divorce out of the picture, maintain and care for your marriage with lots of love just like you would maintain your car with checkups. Sometimes you take it to the repair shop and fix what's wrong. A marriage can be repaired as well. Don't throw in the towel so fast before first making sure you have done all you can to fix it.

Marriage has become more of a process than an institution. Only a person who can adapt to change make a success of it. They are the ones who have a partner that is here today and will be here tomorrow.

And for most of us, the person we marry is the only here-today, here-tomorrow person in our lives. But divorce has become a big moneymaker for lawyers. Statistics shows that almost every second marriage ends in divorce. So it seems as if that here-today, here-tomorrow partner might not be here tomorrow unless we learn to adjust. And men have a lot more adjusting to do than women. They also find it more difficult, not only because they have a lot more to lose in the present forms of marriage, but because they are not so easy-going about change.

A large percent of men dislike change and it has a lot to do with the attitude they have toward marriage. Men welcome some changes. A new car, for instance, or a promotion to a better job in another city. But just try to move the living room furniture around or change your hairstyle.

We need to keep this in mind when our mates criticize us. Many women try to change themselves to please their husbands. It is usually a mistake.

"You talk too much," he will say. "why don't you try letting someone else get a word in once in a while?" Or "Meatloaf again? Don't you know how to make anything else?" And the wife tries to please.

The next time the neighbors come over to play cards, she cuts down her flow of conversation. When their guests leave, her husband says, "What was wrong with you tonight? You sat there like a bump on a log." He had fallen in love with her partly because of her nonstop chatter.

Another woman will start leafing through cookbooks looking for new dishes that will fit in her food budget. But when she starts serving them, her husband protest. "What kind of meal is that to give a hungry man? What about some hamburger once in a while? Or a meatloaf?" He didn't really want a change in menus. He just wanted to fuss a little and throw his weight around.

The only change a man really feels comfortable with in his wife or his marriage is something new and different in their sexual routine now and then. But for the rest, they want their wives and their marriage to conform to the traditional pattern. Most men, but not all, want their marriages, like those of their fathers and grandfathers, to be geared to their needs.

A lot of men think of their wives as replacing their mothers. "The wife becomes a support system. She integrates him, fulfills him, provides a home for him and enables him to be out in the world and feel more secure about himself," say Alan Shanel, a New York psychotherapist. "Many men can function better in the world if they know they have a home behind them. And they do not feel adequate to establish that home themselves."

But not all that many women are interest in life as a support system any more. Women want a husband who will consider them an equal partner, not a kind of privileged domestic. The power struggle that ensues as women claim more rights and power from men who are understandably reluctant to relinquish them has turned many unions into little civil wars that end in mutual secession.

The single greatest change in marriage may be the emergence of the dual-career marriage. There have always been marriages in which both husband and wife worked, but now they are becoming the norm. They represent almost 50 percent of marriages in this marriage. And the men involved are finding them a terra incognita. Unsurveyed and unmapped.

Husbands in dual-career marriages tend to feel cheated. They are not getting the care and attention that their friends and colleagues with nonworking wives enjoy. (Remember, I am speaking in terms of the average husband, not necessarily yours who may be wonderful). Dinner is not on the table when he gets home. He has to rummage through the laundry basket for his socks. The bed is never made. He misses the rapt attention his wife used to pay to his stories of what when on at the office. Now she wants equal time to take about what went on at her office. And she expects him to do the dishes while she puts the children to bed.

Even the men, and I am thinking of the younger men especially, who claim to support the women's movement still expect marriage to revolve around them and their interests, just as their father's marriage revolved around him and his interests. As we know, a man's job is the center of his world.

Studies show that what a man does for a living counts twice as much as his education in his eyes of the world. The Princeton man who works as a golf pro has a lower status than the man who attended a small mid-western college and is president of Amalgamated Corporation. And this extends to wives, as well. Mrs. Princeton may be a highly regarded biochemist, but she is lower in the social pecking order than Mrs. Amalgamated housewife, since even today social status is still keyed to the husband's job. A non-working wife, in fact, is coming to be considered something of a status symbol. Although not by many women. The "just a housewife" tag that some women still use to describe themselves shows how much a status symbol they think they are.

When psychologists compared single-career and dual-career couples in 189 marriages, they discovered that the dual-career husbands did not enjoy life anywhere near as much as the single-career spouses.

Husbands with working wives were worriers. They worried about their health, both physical and mental. They worried about where they were living and whether they should move. They worried that they had fallen in a rut, both in their personal and business lives. They often found it difficult to show affection for their wives and that worried them too.

In their eyes, their masculine self-image was tarnished. The fact that their wives worked meant that they would be pressured into taking over a certain amount of domestic chores—women's work. They loved their wives, but they felt that their marriage were lacking.

The housewives resembled the dual-career husbands in many ways. Their self-esteem was low. They worried about their health and their marriage and their children. They were often seriously depressed.

The single-career husbands had their own worries, but these were of a different order from those of the men married to working wives. The single-career husbands worried about inflation, the possibility of war, racial violence, the energy crisis, the stock market. But their worries seldom kept them awake nights. They felt in robust good health. They looked forward to each new day and welcomed its challenges. And they considered themselves happily married.

The dual-career wives were much like the single-career husbands. They had plenty of confidence in themselves. They were happy and healthy. They felt good about their jobs and their marriages. And they did not worry all that much.

A divorce lawyer who has presided over the dissolution of many dual-career marriages comments that "while there are undoubted many marriages that have been strengthened when a wife works, the ones I see in my practice are the others. It takes a monumentally self-assured man not to be intimidated by his wife's success in a area he was raised to regard as his alone."

It is even difficult for men to come to terms with the reasons their wives work. Three out of five wives work, according to a survey by the A.C. Nielson people, because the family needed the money or they wanted money for extras—summer camp for the kids, a second car, a new kitchen, a family vacation. Only 19 percent of the women queried said that they worked because they wanted to. Only 29 percent said that the family needed the second income.

Several major advertising agencies did studies of dual-career marriages to ascertain just how much husbands participated in the running of the household. And all the surveys came up with the same finding. Men did a lot more talking about helping than actual helping. Eighty percent of the men questioned in one survey said that even though their wife worked full time, they expected her to take full responsibility for the household, the shopping, and the children. "Today's man may be sympathetic to the fact that this is a tough juggling act," the Batten, Barton, Durstine and Osborne study commented, "yet the majority are not willing to lift the traditional household responsibilities from their wives.

Thirty-five percent of the husbands in the Doyle Dan Bernbach study agreed that vacuuming was an acceptable male chore and not demeaning to the masculine image, but only 27 percent of them had ever pushed a vacuum across the living room rug. "It is easier for men to accept the possibility of women as brain surgeons than to release their own wives from the drudgery of laundry and cleaning the bathroom," the researchers concluded.

Men understand very well that they have as much to lose as their wives have to gain. Women are escaping from the solitary confinement of the home into the office and the laboratory, the sales territory and the stock exchange. They dress better and feel more attractive than when they stayed at home. They meet people. They face challenges. Life becomes exciting. And they get paid for it. The only thing that has not changed is the housework. It is there waiting for them every night. Rings around the tub. Dust kittens under the bed. Dishes in the sink. Even the most reluctant husband finds himself forced to take over some of the domestic chores, if only to make sure he has clean underwear for the next day. But he does the minimum—and usually grudgingly.

The working wife spends an average of twenty-six hours a week on housework; her husband spends thirty-six minutes. Nor do children make much difference in the amount of help a husband gives his wife. A three-year long study of fourteen hundred dual-career marriage with children under eleven years old showed that only one father in five helped out with the youngsters.

The real heroes are the blue-collar husbands of America. They do not talk much about the women's movement and when they do, they do not have much good to say about it, but they pitch in and help their wives more cheerfully and competently than their white-collar neighbors.

Sex in dual-career marriage often becomes as much of a hassle as housework. The demands of a full-time job plus running the household leave many women so deeply fatigues that they have little zest for sex. "If she were seeing another guy," one husband complained, "I'd have a better chance of getting her in bed. She wouldn't want me to suspect that she was fooling around. But what chance do I have against her job? She is a success. And she's crazy about success."

The childless couple can usually avoid the housework and sex hassles because their two incomes give them more financial leeway, but this does not mean that their marriage is stress-free. When there are no children, it is often because the wife is deeply committed to her career. And this commitment often results in husband and wife competing with each other.

The ultimate power in a marriage is decision-making, which has always been the male prerogative. But his is changing too. One study that has been going on for some thirty years has regularly queried a group of twelve hundred women to see how their thinking has changed. Over the years the largest shift has been in their responses to this statement: "Most of the important decisions in the life of the family should be made by the man of house." In 1962, two thirds of the women agreed. By 1977, two thirds of the women disagreed.

The most important decision that faces a husband and wife is probably that of whether or not to have children. Many women are resisting motherhood, especially those who are intent on their careers. They know that if they stay home with their child during those vitally important early years, they are going to fall behind and will probably never regain the momentum they have now, never reach the goals they set for themselves. And yet they are not willing to compromise the future of their child by going back to work immediately. Women today have learned how important it is to be with their child in the early years. They go through harsh soul-searching and agonizing over whether to be pregnant now or later or never. There has recently been an upsurge in the number of women over thirty who are having their first child. "There is a profound baby hunger around these days," one psychiatrist reports, "among women who have put off having children." No one has yet analyzed it carefully, but it may be that these women have come to the decision that children are more important than success. Or they may have discovered that they are not going to reach those hoped-for peaks. So they are now going to have a child before it is too late.

Demographers tell us that 25 percent of couples between twenty-five and twenty-nine will never have children and another 25 percent of this group will settle for having one child.

The decision is easy for men. Many are pressuring their working wives to get pregnant. It is not the old story of "Keep them barefoot and pregnant." Men have gone far beyond that primitive way of thinking. It is simply that men have less to give up than women. The responsibility for the child still falls on the mother.

We hear about young fathers who have become "house husbands" and others who happily share half the care of the baby, but as I travel around the country and talk to young mothers, I find that these men are almost as rare as crow's teeth. The only reason we hear about them is because they are so unusual. There is also an element of wishful thinking involved. By publicizing these men, others may be induced to follow in their footsteps.

Many men who pressure their wives to have a baby end up regretting it. Children place an almost unbearable stress on marriage—all marriages, not only the dual-career marriage. The idea that children strengthen marriage is a joke.

Marriage is changing. The married man no longer thinks of himself as being in the happiest of all situations. According to a Gallup Poll, there are now more happy women than happy men. Almost half the women in this country considered themselves happy, but only about a third of the men do.

With that in mind, it just pretty much tells us something that we all pretty much know and that is the fact that we are all imperfect. But with all the imperfections we can still connect to make our unions last a lifetime, and all it takes is an effort and a mindset to nurture your marriage the same way you would do a flower garden. Without the sunshine, the rain and your care, your flower garden will not survive. The same goes for your marriage. Without the love and care and a real effort to make it work, a marriage will not survive!

Chapter 47

Don't Play the Martyr to Please Him

Who is to say why we really do what we do or how we end up getting caught up in certain situations? But at one point or another in all of our lives, we play the martyr for someone or something, whether it's constantly burning the mid-night oil to please a boss who never gives us a pat on the back; or whether it's breaking your back constantly for someone who never lends a hand or utter a thank you.

Try not to get yourself caught up in playing the martyr, especially to your mate. Because when you play the martyr to please him—you lose yourself. Not to say, many of us don't look forward to giving of ourselves and going that extra mile to make that special man in our lives happy. But when playing the martyr becomes a constant way of behavior, it's time to take a step back and think about if what we're doing is really what we want to do. Because sometimes, no doubt, we can get so caught up into playing the martyr to please someone else that it can become a regular behavior pattern. We find ourselves in a rut, molded in that way of life. Doing things and saying things to a mate that deep down we really don't want to do or say. We can end up losing ourselves and what really counts to us. Because when we play the martyr, chances are we are giving up our own hopes, dreams, wishes and desires in our effort to please and make the man we love happy.

Wanting to make the man in your life happy is a natural loving thing, and it always make us feel better when we make our partner happy, but feeling better can easily turn into feeling worse when you allow your mate's happiness at the cost of your own personality, ambitions, and true desires, allowing your happiness to be pushed aside, like having a pie and giving it all to him.

Six Signs of Playing the Martyr:
Making Sacrifices:
Do you rarely say no and usually agree to do things for your mate even though you know you will resent it later? Do you do whatever he wants you to do even if it is harmful to you? For instances, he asks you to do something that you would never dream of doing, but you go on and do it against your better judgment because doing it will please him.

Depend On Him for Your Happiness:
Do you depend on your mate for your happiness? thinking, I would be happy if only he loved me more/would stop drinking, and so on? Do you hand over to him responsibility for certain aspects of your life? Do you isolate yourself from the support of friends and family because he doesn't like them? And of course, you want to do whatever you can to prevent an argument. Do you ask him for constant reassurance that you are good enough?

Putting Your Mate On a Pedestal:
Do you believe he is much braver, stronger, or better than you are? Do you remain loyal to your mate even after he hurts you? When your mate attacks you, do you speak up for yourself or do you first pause and question yourself rather than question him?

Cowering When Attacked:
Do you whine, nag, and complain about him to others, yet never stand up to him? When family and friends mention his bad behavior, do you right away take his side, making excuses for your mates bad behavior? After a fight or a breakup, do you apologize to him to save the relationship even when you were not at fault?

Do You Express Your Anger?
Do you share your feelings when you're upset with him? For instance, if you're upset about something he said or did, do you confront him

and let him know his words are actions hurt you or you keep your thoughts and sad feelings to yourself because you don't want to hurt his feelings by telling him that he has hurt yours?

Resorting to Passive-Aggressive Behavior:
Instead of expressing your anger directly and letting him know exactly how you feel, do you overdraw the checking account, forget to give him important phone messages, or sabotage him in some other way?

If you answered yes to any of the six signs, you are probably playing the martyr, and when you find yourself engaging in this kind of behavior, you are allowing and even encouraging your mate to behave badly toward you. In a healthy, balanced relationship, our sacrifices and gifts are compromises matched by our mate's. The act of giving should be recognized and appreciated, not expected.

Now you're thinking, "okay, I'm stuck in a rut with this behavior, but what can I do about it?"

Well, to bring an abrupt end to this kind of pattern of playing the martyr, it requires that you drop the illusions, and 101 excuses you have given yourself to do it, and be totally honest with yourself about your situation. You must open your eyes and see it for what it really is. Because deep down, you know if you open your eyes wide enough you'll be able to see the whole picture. The real picture! The one that you may not want to face, so therefore you keep your eyes close. But in order to break free of playing the martyr, you must face the situation and take control of your own thoughts and feelings. And live to bring some happiness toward yourself as well as your mate.

If you find yourself stuck in a rut of playing the martyr, you should tell yourself over and over that you are in charge of your own life and that no one else has a right or a valid reason to treat you badly. Whenever he treats you badly and behaves toward you in a clearly unacceptable manner, bring it straight to his attention. Stand up to him and put your foot down, set boundaries, and follow through with consequences if he crosses them.

Chapter 48

Handling Your Husband's Negative Moods

We all get in a bad mood and lose our composure, screaming and yelling here and there. It's unheard of to never have a bad day. But some of us can have more bad days it seems than other. If your spouse falls into that category you could use a few tips on handling his negative moods and high emotion. What would any of us do when our mate hits an emotional flash point, and feelings such as resentment, anger, depression and anxiety take center stage? Flash points are moments when one spouse is so over-whelmed with bad feelings that their poison spills over onto their partner. Nobody will react well when emotionally blasted in this way; and without a clear map of how to respond, you are likely to make things worse.

Learning to identify what triggers a flash point can often help you see the storm coming and maybe even head it off. At the least, under-standing emotional triggers helps you weather a mate's emotional storm more sympathetically than you otherwise might.

Almost any event—from the trivia of a spilled pudding to the inconvenience of a missed plane to the shock of a sudden job loss can trigger an emotional meltdown for you or your mate. These storms often seem irrational: If you look closely, you'll see that neither your emotional upheavals or your husband's occur as randomly as they might seem to. According to Dr. Judith Sills, a clinical psychologist who practices in Philadelphia. "If you look beneath the incidents, you'll spot the triggers: displaced anxiety, personal frustration and marital hot spots." Once you identify which one has set your husband in a bad mood, you'll find it easier to respond more wisely without setting him off even more.

Displaced Anxiety:

Each of us responds to certain situations with more anxiety than we consciously recognize. When we are in one of these vulnerable situations, we're apt to go over the emotional edge in response to any small setback, but without really understanding why. Any number of situations make people vulnerable to anxiety. Some of us feel it every Sunday night, anticipating the office on Monday. Others rev up every time they entertain or melt down when they see their parents, even though they are parents also.

Do you know which situations make you vulnerable to emotional overload? Can you identify those that set off your husband? If you can say to yourself, "Oh, that's just how he gets because flying makes him nervous," you're less likely to be hurt if he snaps at you. Explaining in advance that you're always blue when the family vacation is over might help him to know how to cheer you up and be less annoyed by your heavy sighs.

Personal Frustration:

This occurs when you have a goal in mind and some obstacle prevents you from reaching it. People whose frustration tolerance is immature, or who have learned to discharge bad feelings by venting them on others, hit the frustration flash point regularly. But all of us can hit it on a bad day. Recognizing your own capacity for frustrated outbursts helps you to ride through his without taking them so personally.

Marital Hot Spots:

These are topics that trigger defensiveness and resentment whenever they come up. Sex, in-laws and money are the big three. They may simmer beneath the surface, then erupt in fury or despair every time they're confronted. Other typical hot spots are disagreements over child rearing, housework, religion or socializing.

Because significant differences in these areas are painful to resolve, many of us bury them, along with our feelings, and avoid situations that will force these issues to surface. For example, we may hide purchases rather than discuss our money differences, or endure unsatisfying sex lives rather than face the painful conversations required to improve things. Avoidance as a strategy is only partially successful though, since it's just a temporary solution and doesn't ease your festering feelings. Eventually, often when you least expect it, the old fight over your mother-in-law comes rushing to the surface and one of you hits a flash point. So what can you do?

Self-Preservation

When your mate's negative emotions spill out over you, you have two goals. To preserve your own well-being. Then, to help him through his tough time.

"Preserve your own well-being" means first and foremost insuring your physical safety. When people lose control of their emotions, they may also lose control of their behavior. If your husband has ever lashed out physically, even once; if he hits, pushes, shoves, or makes physically threatening gestures—the two of you need to talk to a professional counselor.

Second, self-preservation means protecting yourself from your mates anger or miserable mood, which otherwise will be communicated to you. You can take care of yourself by:

- Leave His Presence: Leave the room or house. A few minutes away from his tantrum can help restore your sense of control.

Just because he's throwing around ugly words doesn't mean you have to stand there and catch them.

- Remove Yourself Mentally: When he's cursing another driver and you're in the passenger seat receiving those curses, you can still leave, if only in your mind. Sing "The Star Spangled Banner" to yourself, recite a poem you've memorized, or picture some great time you had with him when he was being his best self. Choose any thought that will help you to feel better.

- Keep Yourself Calm: A mate's emotional meltdown can be scary and trigger your own anxiety. Talk to yourself. Remember that this is temporary, that everyone has bad moments, that you've had a few yourself. Realize that although you're the unlucky audience for his outburst, that doesn't necessarily make you his target.

If his behavior succeeds in making you anxious or angry, you're apt to have a meltdown of your own, so wait until you feel calm, adult and relatively cheerful before offering him assistance. Then try the following:

- Don't Response: When he tosses the blame your way, resist the temptation to defend yourself. Instead, either calmly go on about your business or change the subject ("I think we're going to have a good time tonight, don't you?). Take a moment later on to tell him how his comment made you feel. The best defenses are always strategically timed.

- Fix The Problem: Wade in and try to solve his problem. If you can relieve a frustration, why not do so? When you're cursing because you can't find your keys, isn't it nice when he joins in the search and allows you your crankiness?

- Hear The Fear: Identifying your spouse's stress patterns and your own makes it possible to hear the fear beneath his behavior. If he's yelling for you to hurry up, for instance, it may help him if you label his anxiety: He: "Get a move on. We need to go!" She: "You're going to give a great speech. I've heard it, and I know you're ready."

- Listen Well: Listen without defense to all of his concerns. Start by saying, "Honey, you seem troubled. Tell me what's on your mind." Encourage him to continue by saying, "What else" or "Is there something more?" When he's finished talking, conclude with, "Thanks for telling me" You'd be surprised how much relief comes from simply feeling heard.

- Remind Him: Remind him and yourself of his strengths: When he's freaking out over money, take a moment to acknowledge the excellent way he watches over the family finances. When he's morose over a professional setback, remind him of how resilient he was after the last one.

Every adult occasionally descends to the howl of a frustrated 2-year-old, ricochets with teenage moodiness, or gives vent to an anxious middle-aged whine. These are the moments when you want to cling tight with one hand to your sense of humor and sense of self while stretching out the other hand to support the one you love.

Chapter 49

7 Steps to Reject Depression

A book about making a marriage last a lifetime would not be complete without a chapter about depression. Because no matter how happy we can be at one point, there are times during any marriage would we'll feel down about something—and if the problem is big enough, even downright depressed.

Coming face to face with depression right after losing my brother to lung cancer on Thanksgivings day, 1996, I personally know that it can be a dark, confusing experience. So dark that everything around you seem dim.

Depression didn't knock on my door, it walked right in—in full bloom. I was afraid to be alone, afraid to sleep, afraid to eat, afraid to leave home, afraid of the dark, afraid of people. I knew depression had broken me into many pieces. Some days I felt like it was the beginning of the end of life as I had known it. Nothing seemed important or worthwhile. I just couldn't feel the joy in living. Each day was just like the next, I had no idea how I would break free and make myself whole again. But I was determined not to be swallowed up by depression, and little by little I was able to reject depression with the following steps listed here:

Most of us feel low or sad from time to time, but feeling low or down on occasions doesn't necessary group us into a category of being considered mentally ill, as long as we're able to continue with a daily routine. So, if you or someone in your family has occasional periods of blues that last a few days or weeks, you probably don't have depression. But, on the other hand, when depression seriously start affecting a person's job performance and their personal relationships, psychiatrist consider these individuals to have depression. Such depression may persist, and even deepen, eventually interfering with that person's ability to lead a normal life.

What Is Depression?

Depression is described as an excessive emotional reaction to loss. Sometimes the losses are internal, such as loss of self-esteem or loss of hope. Depression is a normal emotion following the loss of a close relative or a job; it may occur after failure to meet a life goal or during a disabling (and possibly fatal) illness, such as cancer or stroke. This form of depression is known as exogenous, or reactive depression. Usually it just has to be lived through, and it is only when symptoms and feelings persist and continue to interfere with function that it can be characterized as an illness.

We can think we're coping okay after a major emotional incident happens in our lives, but serious depression can start sitting in. We may not figure it out right away, or know exactly what's going on with us, but we'll know something is wrong from our unusual behavior.

According to Dr. Sandra Kahn, a psychotherapist in Chicago, Illinois, author of *The Ex-Wife Syndrome*, Some of us are more susceptible to depression than others. Many people at particular stages in their lives seem especially susceptible to depression. Such as late adolescence, middle age, and the years after retirement. Those are some of the more critical periods. For instances, many of us find the transition from adolescence to adulthood difficult, especially when there are work pressures. In middle age, loss of fertility or virility may seem like loss of sexuality, a loss that can trigger depression; plus, depression itself can cause a loss of interest in sex. Someone in late middle age may brood over the fact that they can no longer advance in their career.

It seems that depression among older people is extremely common. This may be related to their recognition of certain physical limitations that comes along with aging, and the realization that death is in the foreseeable future.

Symptoms of Depression

It is common to become apathetic about the outside world or withdrawn. It is also common to have difficulty concentrating. It's common to lose interest in or have trouble with sex, eating and sleeping. Certain individuals may experience problems with indigestion, constipation, and even headaches. You may be preoccupied with your body and have imaginary physical illness. All depressed individuals have severe psychological symptoms, and some may lose touch with reality, feeling guilty and worthless without cause, and may even believe that they are being persecuted, and may have hallucinations.

The Intensity of some of the symptoms you may experience often varies with the time of day. For instances, typically, someone who is depressed wakes up early with almost no mental energy, but improves as the day progresses. On the other hand, some people have their worst symptoms at night. This disorder progresses, the depression may deepen until it never lifts. In a case like that, the person then becomes totally withdrawn and may spend most of their time in bed.

7 Steps Toward Rejecting Depression

Regular Exercise:
Recent research has proved that exercise actually produces chemicals that reduce depression. Choose your form of exercise to match your state of health and physical abilities. If you are in good health, jogging, swimming, or aerobics will help you the most in combating depression. If age or health is a limiting factor, though, try brisk

walking. Such physical activities will not only help you with depression but will contribute to your overall health and put you in touch with others.

Proper Diet:

Rigorously limit your dietary intake of sugars, other carbohydrates, and caffeine, and bulk up your protein intake. Eating large amounts of sugar creates a short-term increase in the blood-sugar level, which you might experience as a temporary bust of energy. After the burst, however, you'll experience a dramatic decline in blood sugar, which can contribute substantially to a feeling of depression. To avoid such chemically induced mood swings, eliminate that morning sweet roll or doughnut and forget about candy and chocolate for a while. Also, put some effort into curbing other carbohydrate intake such a high-carbohydrate diet can intensify fluctuations in your blood-sugar level throughout the day. Toast and orange juice (both high-carbohydrate foods) will start your day by putting you on the same roller coaster as a doughnut will. To achieve what control you can over your emotional state, combine your carbohydrates with foods that are high in protein such as eggs, cheese, meats, and nuts. Pay attention to your cholesterol intake, which proteins tend to boost, and try to balance the decrease in sugars and carbohydrates with an increase in protein since your system breaks down protein fastest when you are under stress.

Limit Caffeine:

Caffeine stimulates both the central nervous system and the liver. The result of liver stimulation is a surge of glucose in the bloodstream, followed, in about an hour and a half, by a steep drop in blood sugar that can contribute to depression. Do your self a favor and strictly limit your caffeine intake.

Limit Alcohol:

Limit alcohol and avoid drugs. Many people are unaware that alcohol is a depressant. It might make you feel good for a brief period, but the high will inevitably be followed by a low, even more extreme than the one with which you started. Other drugs will anesthetize you emotionally for a time and/or confuse you. The last thing you need to contend with in fighting off depression is a chemically induced distortion of reality.

Monitoring Your Depression:
If you find that your depression doesn't lift or that it is regularly accompanied by thoughts of suicide, you should seek a doctor.

Self-Help:
Keeping busy—including a vacation, a hobby, or sports—may help you pull out of a mild depression, as may spending time with others.

Professional Help:
This depends on the type and severity of symptoms. If you go to your doctor with symptoms of depression, he or she may refer you to a psychiatrist. And treatment may consist of medication, psychotherapy, or a combination of both. Antidepressants, which are often used in treatment of depression, can usually begin to provide relief within 2 to 3 weeks. In severe cases a psychiatrist should always be involved.

Chapter 50

5 Special Ways to Rekindle Your Lovelife

Rekindle your lovelife by allowing your marriage to blossom pro-fusely at the hand of romance. Even if you're not a true romantic, you can still live as a romantic and think as a romantic. By allowing your-self to bring this kind of mindset into your relationship, it will not only help to strengthened the foundation of your union, it will bring more excitement into yours and your partner's life. Plus when you indulge your relationship in romance, you live free from the burden of **boredom** stepping in and ripping your love into threads.

Tips To Help Rekindle Your Love Life

The key word here, is to be creative. Creative with music, candles and lighting to name a few. Romantics are creative. They see their rela-tionships as opportunities to express their creativity, as arenas for self-expression, as safe havens for experimenting, and as places for growth.

Romantic Mornings:

Romantic mornings can get your day off to a delicious start. Set you're the alarm clock early enough to spend at least an hour or so together before heading off to work. Enjoy morning love and start the day with tons of energy. Share a light breakfast in bed after the love-making. Or better yet, throw on your robe and light a candle at the kitchen table. It doesn't matter what you're serving, whether it's French toast and hash browns or just a bowl of cold cereal. The idea is to sit there together and enjoy it. Sharing a meal right after lovemaking have a way of giving a couple instant energy. Don't be surprise if you pay another visit to the bedroom before your two hours are up.

Romantic Dinners:
Have him come home to a romantic meal. Light the sweet smelling candles before he arrives and set the mood by dimming the lights and having his favorite music playing in the background. Use your best china even if you're only serving a grilled cheese sandwich and French fries. If you have a full work schedule as he does, you won't always have the luxury of time/energy to cook a full course candle light dinner at your place, but keep romantic candlelit dinners on the agenda for those occasions when you do feel fully rested. But during one of your romantic evening while dinning out, add a little mystery to the setting. "Hide a very small gift somewhere on your body. Then say to your lover, "I've got a gift for you, and it's hidden on me somewhere! Find it and it's yours!" Use your imagination—and be sure to leave enough time to participate in any "extracurricular activities" that may result from the search.

Romantic Fantasies:
As long as you feel comfortable with it, try and make one of his fantasies come true and that will surely drive him absolutely wild. "Sharing a fantasy can be the height of intimacy. Fantasies are your most guarded secret and vulnerable thoughts. Fantasy is a chance to play, to indulge yourself and your partner in pleasure. There's an innocence in fantasy, a winning foolishness that dares to be silly or ridiculous. Yet because fantasies are so private, you need trust to share them. You need to enter into and share fantasies cautiously, one step at a time," says Dr. Phillips.

Romantic Evenings:
Allow no excuse to stop your evenings out with your spouse. You may look at your desk and all the work piled high, and think to yourself, "I got to call him and cancel. I got to mark this evening off the calendar.

There's no way I can squeeze in the time to go to the movies with him. How can I get a baby-sitter at this short notice? But you can find a babysitter just like you know your work will be waiting for you the next day. So let nothing stop you from setting aside an evening out for you both. Try for once a week, twice a week is even better, giving the two of you time out on the town, enjoying and discovering new places and things to do together. All too often after a couple has been married for awhile or has dated for awhile—spending evenings out together get marked off of the list for one reason or another. One or the other decides there's no fun in eating out, the movies, dancing or doing anything outside of their four walls. They have each other and they feel they don't need anything else. But that's the wrong frame of mind. That frame of mind has watched many couples march into divorce court and say good-bye to what they thought was a solid union. Couples need the excitement and the adventure of doing things together. Those who lean toward no fun time, they also lean toward building a split in their love foundation. Make an all out effort toward spending an evening out. The outings will serve as much needed glue in keeping the romance in your marriage.

Romantic Lingerie:

When we first say "I do", we want to look our sexy best and we run out to lingerie stores looking for sexy outfits, but after the newness of the marriage wears off, we tend to just settle for that comfortable old gown that we can't resist reaching for. You know the one I'm talking about, the one we know we should throw out, but we keep holding on to anyway. Make an effort to throw out those old comfortable rags. They may be comfortable to us, but they are an eye sore to him. A new sexy nightie can be just as comfortable. Wear lingerie even if you're not in the mood. Often just wearing something sexy can turn you on. Even if you have sexy night wear, it wouldn't hurt to invest in your lingerie wardrobe every once in awhile, buying rich bold colors like radiant red, bright yellow and shiny black. And another suggestion to consider, if you wear long gowns, try short ones; and if you always buy cotton and polyester, try nylon, silk or satin; and if your night wear is traditional, try exotic items.

Chapter 51

8 Ways to Know Your Love Is On the Rocks

Ever hear the expression "Throwing good money after bad?" Of course you have. It comes to mind every time you shell out more money to repair (again!) that old wreck of a car you've been meaning to get rid of. You toss good money into the bottomless pit of repairs and you know there's no end in sight. As far as that car is concerned, it's just, "Patch, patch, patch!"

Well, it's the same with relationships. When a relationship reaches the point where you're just tossing good intentions and tender emotions into a bottomless pit of misery, boredom and unhappiness, then perhaps it's time to move on. Get going while the going is good, cause the staying is going to be terrible!

But how do you know when it's time for a change? Here is a simple and simplified checklist. Obviously the choice to end a relationship is complex and the point here is by no means to minimize that agonizing decision, but if more than three of the following apply to your situation, maybe, just maybe, it's over!

Nothing Helps:

You've tried everything to improve your relationship and nothing helps. You've talked, you've listened, you've sought help and advice, you've followed the experts, you've been patient and hard working, but no matter what, your relationship hasn't improved. The activities you two used to share, the moments that used to be full of pleasure and promise have taken on the heaviness of chores. If you've really done your utmost to improve your relationship and nothing has worked, then maybe it's time to move on.

Loss of Focus:

One sure sign of being in love is thinking of nothing but your beloved. You want to be with him, you can't wait to see him, can't wait to tell him this, and can't wait to get his reaction to that. Love is the most delicious kind of anticipation. A sure sign that the bloom is off the rose is when your focus totally shifts and that anticipation is replaced by dread. Or maybe it's just that suddenly everything other than your relationship seems more exciting. It could be a sign that you have fallen out of love.

No Time for Love:

Is the idea of spending more time in the bedroom the last thing on your mind? Does it suddenly seem that there's no time for romance and not much desire either? Has sex become a meaningless ritual, rather than an expression of a shared bond? And again, as mentioned at the start, have you tried everything to revitalize this vital part of your relationship? If you have answered "yes" to these questions, your relationship is very possibly over. Sad to admit, but that may be the case.

That Old Tired Feeling:

You keep asking yourself, where have all the good times gone? And why is everything you do together either stressful or deadly boring? Sitting together watching TV is no longer relaxing, it's as tension-filled as an argument—even when nothing is said. Going out to dinner sounds like it's going to be fun, but in reality turns out to be dull. Parties and dances can still be fun, but only if you find someone to talk to who is more interesting than your man. Somehow, there's no glitter in the relationship any more. It's not that you feel physically old and tired, it's more like feeling drained and dry and dusty. Not a good feeling; not a good sign.

Silence Is Not Golden:

When communication stops, so does the affair. If you no longer have the urge to share information, then forget about it! Without communication, without the simple back-and-forth of talking things over, problems have no solutions. If you and he no longer care what the other is thinking or feeling, or if you have lost the trust that makes it possible to be honest with each other, then as far as your personal Love Boat is concerned, the ship has sailed! if sex is the dessert in a relationship, then communication is the meat and potatoes; and sex without communication has only half the bounce.

You Have a Choice:

In your relationship you suddenly feel you've lost all your choices. The sparkle and spontaneity of your early days together have been replaced by feelings of obligation. It's no longer the life together you want to live, it's the only life that seems possible with him, and it's no longer fun, satisfying or meaningful. Looking forward to your next time with him, you suddenly realize you'd rather be somewhere else, doing anything else. You feel you're stuck in an emotional rut. Your own good sense is telling you this relationship has had it! Follow your gut. Throw in the towel, if that's going to make you happy.

Why Bother?

When you stop caring about how you look for the man you're with, watch out! Chances are your love is fading fast, and probably his too. When we're in love, naturally we want to look our best for that special guy. We present ourselves in a manner designed to please him. When looking our best doesn't seem worth the effort, why bother? If we've stopped caring about whether he likes what we wear or how we look, then, maybe, we've also stopped caring about him.

Love Is Not That Loud:

Every relationship has it ups and downs, it's disagreements and lovers' spats. There's even room in a loving relationship for a good old-fashioned quarrel. But when you find that you are constantly at each other's throats over every little thing, when the noise level reaches the point where the neighbors know just as much about your problems as you do, then it's time to turn down the volume. Love isn't that loud! And it goes without saying, if physical violence has entered the picture, you should be out that door and fast!

For the last word on this subject, let's rephrase the idea we started out with. When a relationship is in trouble, it's important to try to fix it, but it's also important to know when to walk away. Here's to a new beginning!

Chapter 52

7 Women Tell Why They Left

Chances are you or someone you know has dropped a bomb on someone for one reason or another. You found yourselves in a situation where you thought your relationship was cool, but just like that you end up dropping a bomb on your man and called it quits! Sometimes he found out why you left, and sometimes he never got a straight answer, if any answer at all.

There are no guarantees in life. Not one single certainty. Like I used to hear my mother say, we are sure of only two things in this life: taxes and death. And there are certainly no guarantees in a relationship. It doesn't matter whether he just took you out on a first date or whether the two of you have enjoyed thousands of dates. The bottom line is still the same. Being in any love affair is a gamble. It's like the roll of a dice or the flip of a card, sometimes you win and sometimes you lose. But regardless to the tragedy of losing, most individuals would agree that the most important part is if you play the game! There's a saying that it's better to have loved and lost than to not have loved at all. But why do some women suddenly walk away from their relationships without a note or an explanation to their man? Listen in as they tell all…

Cheating Heart:

Janice, Supermarket Worker, 44:

"I broke up with my last boy friend and walked away from a three year relationship, because frankly I couldn't put up with his fooling around anymore. We lived together and there was something about him that always made me feel that he had been with some other woman. I couldn't put my finger on it, but my gut told me he was cheating on me. For the whole three-years that we were together, I had a hunch that he had a thing for our next-door neighbor's 22-year-old daughter. But I wasn't sure. And even if he did have a crush on her, she had a boy who she seemed crazy about. And I figured a pretty young thing like her would never give some 53-year-old guy like Buddy the time of day. but I finally ate those words this past June, when I came home for lunch one Saturday and saw him through the kitchen window performing oral sex on her. I never did mention that incident; I was hurt, but I wasn't surprised. I had figured he was cheating. Without any explanations to him as to why I was moving out, I hightailed it out of his house the next day."

Lack of Acceptance:

Gail, Cocktail Waitress, 26:

"He was a big time executive with a huge corporation; and I was proud of his work, and told him on many occasions. But he was ashamed of my work, and didn't accept it as a real job. He knew I was a waitress and loved my job when he first asked me out; but all while I was going out with him, the main topic of conversation would be about me finding another job. No matter how I explained how much I enjoyed my work, he would not accept me at my word. He figured I couldn't be satisfied being a waitress. I was satisfied and I got tired of him making me feel beneath him. I loved him and it was hard on me, but I broke off with him by not seeing him or returning any of his calls. Our six-month affair was all about him making me feel like I had to change in order to get his true love and affection. He straight out said to me, "Gail, when you can find a better paying job, we can start talking about our future." In other words, as long as I was a waitress we didn't have a future with each other. Maybe in the end, he figured out why I stopped seeing him, if not, too bad. I didn't need some jerk who couldn't accept me."

Already Involved/Lonely:

Elaine, School Bus Driver, 37:

"I walked away from my relationship suddenly without a word to Jerome as to why I was not going to see him again. When I was younger and used to hear about these kinds of things happening, I wondered how could someone just pick up and leave the next person without a word. My Aunt Maxine packed her bags and left my Uncle Hal while he was at work one day. He never heard from her again. It's no longer a mystery to me since I'm one of those people who suddenly walked away. In my situation, the relationship was never really supposed to happen. I was the culprit in this affair. I was already involved. I had a boyfriend overseas. But I didn't tell my boyfriend (of three years) overseas or my new boyfriend (of three months) that there were someone else in the picture. I knew Jim would be away for the next four months, and I just couldn't do that waiting game. I couldn't stand being all alone and lonely. So I got involved with another guy. Someone sweet and kind, but when my boyfriend came home, I made up some lame excuse and told the other guy I couldn't go out with him anymore.

Selfishness/Controlling Ways:

Cathy, Secretary, 27:

"Selfishness is the key word here! There are no bones about it. My mother and older relatives thought Matthew was God gift to women, and said I was nuts breaking off with him. My mother loved him because he was doing with his life what she had always wanted from my late father. Matthew was an engineer—making six figures. My first boyfriend with a college education and a decent job and who wanted something. And believe me, just like my Mom, I was pretty strung out over him. I but we couldn't make it. Believe me, it was much more to it than this, but I left his butt because everything had to be his way or the highway. We had to go to all the places he wanted to go and do all the things he wanted to do. He would always ask me, what you want to do? Where you want to go? But when I made suggestions, he always found something wrong with the places I picked."

Jealous Heart:

Paula, Nurse, 35:

"I had a-ways thought that older men was more stable and sure of themselves, but my 56-year-old ex wasn't. He was very good-looking and well built for his age, but he was too damn jealous to stay with. Shortly after his divorce, we lived to together in my apartment for two years, and I swear I don't know how I stuck it out that long! He was so jealous, he didn't even want me to casually glance at or even speak to in passing another man. He had to be by my side at all times and when I wasn't with him he wanted to know every move I had made the moment I left him until the moment I returned. If a wrong number came through, he felt I knew the caller, if I looked out of the passenger's window while going for a drive with him, he felt I knew the man in the passing car. He would pick fights with other men when we went out together if some guy even looked my way. He was a jealous fool and I was afraid he was going to become violent! I kicked him out of my apartment."

Didn't Want Marriage:

Kelly, Banker, 38:

"He was a divorced man, and had just recently divorced, but I expressed my interest in getting married at the beginning of our relationship. He said he felt strongly about remarrying when the right woman came along. After a year and a half of going strong together, I thought maybe he felt I was the right woman. But I found out the hard way that I wasn't, because he never asked me to marry him. I kept bringing up the subject and he kept avoiding it. I wasn't getting any younger. I wanted a husband. I left his butt and never told him why. But I'm pretty sure he figured it out. The last I heard he was still single and playing the field, probably with someone else who thinks he's going to pop the question, but he never will."

Wouldn't Keep A Job:

Faye, Student, 24:

"I was head-over-heels for the last boyfriend I dumped. I had no other choice, though. He would never keep a job. We met at school. I'm still in college and he graduated last year, and since that time he has gone through four different jobs. I mean decent jobs, paying well. But he find something wrong with each one. And what upsets me more than anything is the fact that his Mom worked hard to put him through school, and now she's really ill. She need his financial support. But of course, he doesn't have a job, so that's his excuse.

And the bottom line with our situation is about the same, he was always broke between jobs and borrowing from me. We couldn't have a regular relationship because he never had any money to do anything with. I still care about him, and who knows what may happen if he gets his act together. But right now, he's out of my hair now."

Chapter 53

How to Leave a Fading Love

Sometimes when a marriage/relationship come tumbling down around you, it's just like watching a radiant rose wither right before your eyes—and it seems that no amount of rain or sunshine can save it. It's not always that easy to decide how bad does a relationship have to be before getting out is the only answer. Four questions to help readers diagnose their own situation:

- Is he questioning your opinion to the point where you doubt yourself?

- Does he bombard you with arguments on even the most insignificant issues.

- Does he dismiss your attempts to voice your concerns?

- Do you often suspect, even over trivial matters, that he's lying to you?

It's not always cut and dry where the bad in your marriage/relationship out weigh the good. But one thing for sure is your heart knows. And if the bad is so bad that it overshadows the good? Then maybe it's time to move on.

In some instances, once a person has made up their mind to end a bad marriage/relationship, they will agonize over their decision for weeks, or months or even years before coming to terms with themselves and being brave enough to walk out the door and start a fresh new life. It's important to take all the time you need to get clear about your situation and to test out how much potential your marriage has for change. And many times, the indecisiveness to walk out the door is because their great fear of leaving overshadows their good sense to know they'll be better off if they do.

Important Tips To Consider

Prepare:
Once you get that nagging feeling in the back of your mind, and from what you can also see, that your marriage or relationship is slipping toward the dangerous zone, don't hesitate to start preparing yourself to live without your mate or love interest. For example: If you're not working, get a job. If you can't drive, learn how. If you don't have any financial resources, start putting aside a few dollars out of your pay here and there. Get out there and do what you need to do in order to survive on your own. And if by chance, the two of you are able to come to an understanding and remain together—you'll just be a little bit more independent and a little bit more richer!

Know Your Limits:
What you will and will not accept or put up with in your marriage or relationship. Clarify your bottom line. what are your deepest values and beliefs about what you expect from or deserve in your marriage? How far can you depart from these? At what point do you say, enough! And refuse to continue with business as usual until a change occurs? There is no "right" bottom line for all women. But if you have no bottom line [there's just no way I can leave him until the children are grown], your marriage and self-respect will be severely compromised.

Be Honest:
People appreciate honesty if it's expressed with tact and sensitivity, because that way, they know where they stand. Explain how you no longer want to be apart of the relationship. A relationship that isn't working and only seems to deteriorate more and more each day. And

you don't have to go into the how's and why's, because just as clearly as you can see the relationship/ marriage isn't working—he can see it too.

Expect Some Pain:
Accept that it will be painful; there's no avoiding it. So regardless to how bad a marriage or relationship is, it has been apart of your life and once you walk away it will be painful to some extent. For some more than others. It depends on what kind of falling out the two of you had.

Stay Close With Family/Friends:
You will need their support. Create a rich and enduring network of relationships. You will obviously need the support of friends, family, and community if your marriage ends. If you're isolated or cut off, your marriage will be all the more intense and overloaded. Strengthen your connections to the important people in your life.

Don't Give In To Loneliness:
Once you have made the break, and loneliness sets in, don't allow yourself to feel down-hearted because you haven't been lucky enough to meet another man that you really would like to spend time with.

Recognize that you are going to miss him and that when you do, you'll zoom in on the high points of the relationship and be tempted to return.

When You Have Thoughts of Returning:
If you have thoughts of wanting to return to a heart-draining relationship that took forever to get out of, think long and hard. Think of all the reasons you left in the first place. Think about if you did return—would things be any difference?

Some possible fears that could keep someone stuck in a heart draining marriage/relationship:

- You're afraid you won't survive financially.
- You're afraid the kids will hate you for leaving Dad.
- You're afraid of being alone.
- You keep telling yourself he'll change one day.
- You feel a lousy man is better than no man.
- You feel your family will think you're a failure.
- You feel you have too much too lose (materially).

Life is too short to worry and too beautiful to waste. You have one live to life! Live it to the fullest! Don't worry and waste your life over a marriage/relationship that you have given your all and the holes are still there.

Chapter 54

How to Get Over Losing Him

Being in love and losing that person through the breakup of a love affair or the breakup of a marriage is probably the most burning hurt any individual could ever face. It's worse than losing someone to death. When someone you loves passes away, the pain is crushing, it finds a home within you. It's final. But the breakup of a relationship or marriage doesn't seem final because that person is still out there somewhere having a life, but just not with you.

When the man you love suddenly walks out of your life, the pain is similar to a burning, stabbing feeling right in the middle of your heart. The shock of his leaving will sink in and sock you like a sharp punch in the stomach. And even though, the realization of a lost love is devastating, if we stop and think, we would probably be able to recollect some hints of problems. Because most relationships don't just come tumbling down suddenly, there's usually a few signs, if not a whole ton of signs that your relationship is headed toward trouble. But still just the same, when it happens, we never expect it. You may ask yourself over and over in your head, "What did I say or what did I do wrong to drive him away?" When you find yourself asking that question, turn it around and say instead: "What did he do wrong?" In any relationship, two people have always participated. There are neither saints nor sinners. And most love relationships do not break up in one day. Usually there have been a number of partial breakups, dis-satisfactions that go unresolved until a time comes when the distancing has gone on too long and the whole relationship unravels. The rejected person often looks first for blame in her—or himself, when in fact neither party should shoulder all the responsibility.

The Denial Stage:

In the beginning you are likely to go into denial. The conscious attempt to suppress or screen out the awareness of an unpleasant reality by refusing to believe it or face it. In your heart you still believes he loves you and want you back. You feel it's not over. But when days turn into weeks and weeks turn into months, the cold hard facts hit you. He's gone for good.

Try To Make Amends:

If you decide to try and make amends, put forth a good effort, let him know you still love him and want the relationship, and if he chooses not to reconcile, you'll know you did what you could to try to make amends. But in your efforts to pick up the pieces of your broken heart and mend them back together by falling back into his arms, keep in touch with the reality of why the relationship fail in the first place. Try not to rationalization or suppress the real reasons for the breakup. After it sinks in that he has really walked out of your life, even though, the breakup may be the best thing that could have happened, (maybe he wasn't too good to you. Maybe you weren't that happy with him) you may suppress the bad times between the two of you and think of only the good. Using selective memory, which filters out all the more unpleasant facts. And by doing so, your reality is distorted by sup-pression, and therefore, you are unable to complete the grieving process and move on with your life.

Getting On With Your Life:

Getting on with your life won't be easy. And it mostly depends on the kind of falling out the two of you had. "It's hard to find the strength to walk alone again, to rely on your own resources. But you don't have to do it all by yourself. because your grief springs from the loss of a human being, you need at least one other person to help you bounce back. Friends, therapy, support groups, and group therapy are vitally important at this time. Statistically it has been demonstrated time and again that people who have social and emotional contacts have a better chance of recovery from both psychological and physical problems.

Period of Mourning:

It will seem like an eternity and nothing will seem to ease your agony and loneliness of missing. That void will be there as noticeable as the fingers on your hands. And as the days seem longer and the nights two-fold, time will soon embrace you with relief. Yes, time, it's the only true mender of a broken heart. That's why it's important to throw yourself into some kind of hobby or activity. The hobbies and activities will fill your empty days and help you manage through each one; and with time the hurt and pain will leave you. "It's important to view this as a period of mourning. The length of time it takes will depend upon how much you have emotionally in vested. If you were banking on spending the rest of your life with this man—perhaps even making big personal sacrifices—then you've made an enormous commitment. On the other hand, you might have known someone a long time but invested little effort. That loss won't mean much to you. But above all, the better your self-esteem, the quicker you'll get over him. Those plagued with self-doubt, who still feel lost and vulnerable, can take much longer to get back on track.

Don't Rush Into Another Relationship:

Many people say that the best way to get over one man is to start going out with another one. And that may work for some, but that's called a rebound affair, and most likely it's not going to work out. Because when you just break up with someone who meant the world to you, or even if they didn't mean the world to you, they shared your world for a period of time. You need time to get over that person. In order to mourn, you have to experience the wide range of feelings that accompany loss. Leaping immediately into another love relationship to obliterate the pain of the last one can be an act of desperation. You're still comparing, still trying to find the old person. In fact, impulsively seizing on a new relationship can be a sign that you haven't really gotten over your loss.

Give yourself time to get over him, then move on. You're beautiful and life is short. But don't grieve too long. And don't allow yourself to fall into the trap of displacement. Displacement is assigning the blame for one's negative feelings to a person other than the one responsible. In other words, don't put another guy in the shoes of your ex-love. By doing so, you can shut yourself off from happiness, thinking all guys are this way or that way. It prevents you from expressing and resolving your terrible anger at the real culprit, not the nice fellow who just asked you out.

We all want to love and to be loved. But love makes no promises if you take it off the shelf. Sometimes, it can leave without the blink of an eye. But it's radiance is so beautiful that it's better to have loved and lost to have not loved at all. And when we lose love, there's always someone else waiting in the future to embrace us, and when you can accept your own strengths and limitations, and stop idealizing your lost love, you will be ready to love again.

Conclusion

Loving someone and showing that person how you care should be the easiest task you would ever undertake. This guide was written to take you to the heart of putting together a meaningful marriage or relationship. It will take you down a road toward endless borders of sizzling passion and overwhelming understanding. It brings out a very important point of how men and women express their feelings in different ways. The key is to express that love to your mate in a way that he can understand.

Sometimes your best intentions can go un-noticed by the person that you want to notice. This happens when you express yourself in a way that you understand but your mate does not. If he doesn't realize you are reaching out to show you care, then the two of you are not making a connection.

The African-American Woman's Guide to Great Sex, Happiness and Marital Bliss will help you make that connection. I have given you ideas and suggestions on how to work together and express your love in a way that your mate will receive the message.

Not every suggestion, or every piece of advice, or every line you read will be suited for you; but maybe just one will be the jolt your marriage or relationship needs to get back on track and piece your foundation back together toward the splendor and passion that it craves.

Stay United
Jel D. Lewis (Jones)

ORDER FORM

WWW.AMBERBOOKS.COM
African-American Self Help and Career Books

Fax Orders: 480-283-0991

Telephone Orders: 480-460-1660

Online Orders: E-mail: Amberbks@aol.com

Postal Orders: Send Checks & Money Orders to:

Amber Books Publishing

1334 E. Chandler Blvd., Suite 5-D67

Phoenix, AZ 85048

_____ *The African-American Woman's Guide to Great Sex, Happiness, & Marital Bliss*

_____ *The Afrocentric Bride: A Style Guide*

_____ *Beautiful Black Hair: A Step-by-Step Instructional Guide*

_____ *How to Get Rich When You Ain't Got Nothing*

_____ *The African-American Job Seeker's Guide to Successful Employment*

_____ *The African-American Travel Guide*

_____ *Suge Knight: The Rise, Fall, and Rise of Death Row Records*

_____ *The African-American Teenagers Guide to Personal Growth, Health, Safety, Sex and Survival*

_____ *Get That Cutie in Commercials, Televisions, Films & Videos*

_____ *Wake Up and Smell the Dollars! Whose Inner City is This Anyway?*

_____ *How to Own and Operate Your Home Day Care Business Successfully Without Going Nuts!*

_____ *The African-American Woman's Guide to Successful Make-up and Skin Care*

_____ *How to Play the Sports Recruiting Game and Get an Athletic Scholarship: The Handbook and Guide to Success for the African-American High School Student-Athlete*

_____ *Is Modeling for You? The Handbook and Guide for the Young Aspiring Black Model*

Name:_____

Company Name:_____

Address:_____

City:_____State:_____Zip:_____

Telephone: (_____) _____E-mail:_____

For Bulk Rates Call: **480-460-1660**   ## ORDER NOW

Great Sex	$14.95	☐ Check ☐ Money Order ☐ Cashiers Check
The Afrocentric Bride	$16.95	☐ Credit Card: ☐ MC ☐ Visa ☐ Amex ☐ Discover
Beautiful Black Hair	$16.95	
How to Get Rich	$14.95	CC#_____
Job Seeker's Guide	$14.95	
Travel Guide	$14.95	Expiration Date:_____
Suge Knight	$21.95	
Teenagers Guide	$19.95	**Payable to:**
Cutie in Commercials	$16.95	Amber Books
Wake Up & Smell the Dollars	$18.95	1334 E. Chandler Blvd., Suite 5-D67
Home Day Care	$12.95	Phoenix, AZ 85048
Successful Make-up	$14.95	**Shipping:** $5.00 per book. Allow 7 days for delivery.
Sports Recruiting:	$12.95	**Sales Tax:** Add 7.05% to books shipped to Arizona addres
Modeling:	$14.95	**Total enclosed: $**_____

About the Author

Jel D. Lewis (Jones) has written and published over 100 short stories for college publications and romance magazines and nearly 200 feature articles on relationships, health, beauty, nutrition, travel and teens for leading magazines and online publications.

Currently a resident of Schaumberg, Illinois, Ms. Lewis (Jones) is a graduate of Marion College (Chicago).

When a woman is in love, her entire system becomes alert. She reaches peaks she otherwise never would have reached. Love nourishes her. No other experience is as deep and pleasing.

   —Dr. Grace Cornish, author of *10 Bad Choices That Ruin Black Women's Lives* and *You Deserve Healthy Love, Sis: The Seven Steps to Getting the Relationship You Want*

Model: Jacinta "Gigi" Mercier